How To Create Fun For Children With Disabilities On The Ski Slopes

KONNECT WITH KIDS

SKIING

Dr. Herbert K. Naito

508 West 26th Street KEARNEY, NE 68848
402-819-3224
info@medialiteraryexcellence.com

Table of Contents

Acknowledgements

I want to graciously thank Joseph Huber for the scrutinizing review of this book, Jennifer Barnwell for her gifted talents with her camera, and Jon Stepelton for his graphic artistry.

VAIL Resorts Staff:

Joseph Huber   PSIA Alpine, Level II; PSIA Adaptive, Level II, PSIA Telemark, Level I, PSIA Children's Specialist, Level 2; PSIA Senior Specialist, Level I; Trainer Accreditation; Former Member of PSIA-Central Adaptive Ed Staff.

Local Ski School Photographer:

Jennifer Barnwell   PSIA Alpine, Level I; PSIA Children's Specialist, Level 1

Graphic Artist:

Jon Stepelton   PSIA Alpine, Level 3; PSIA Children's Specialist, Level 2; PSIA; Telemark, Level 3; Alpine, Level 3 Trainer; Vail Resorts Ed Staff

This book was supported by a grant from the Dr. and Mrs. Herbert K. Naito Charitable Foundation.

Something About The Author

He spent 40 years in the medical profession. For fun, he coached skiing for over 20 years. He is a member of the Professional Ski Instructors of America, and is certified in Alpine Skiing, Level 2; Adaptive Specialist, Level 1; Children's Specialist, Level 2; and Children's Trainer. Currently he is employed by the Vail Resorts and is presently on the Vail Educational Staff. He was the former Director of the Children's Advanced Training Specialist, and the Express Pre-School Ski School Programs. In addition to this book, he has written six other books on alpine skiing.

"A Comprehensive Guide for Coaching Children How to Ski"

"How to Prepare for your Child's First Ski Lesson"

"The Funky Donkey Tells His Story About His First Ski Lesson On Safety"

"Coaching Wacky Raccoon, Children, and Adults The Fundamentals Of Good Sportsmanship"

"The Hidden Secrets and Treasures of Having Fun At and Around The Ski Resorts"

"How to Create a Successful Ski Lesson for Senior Citizens"

Chapter 1
Introduction

Every person is special. Children with a disability are extra special because they pursue their dreams with their heart, despite their cognitive, emotional, physical limitations. Many have lofty goals, like going to the Special Olympics and winning medals. They have grit and determination that you can only admire and envy. They put in extra-long practice hours to succeed. They are extra appreciative of their accomplishments. Therefore, it is a delight to work with them.

You may need extra special equipment and ski tools to assist them to 'ski', which I'll discuss later. Adaptive knowledge[1-3] and student's profile are so paramount for the coaches in order to succeed. In addition, the ski instructor needs to be creative and inject *fun* into their lesson plans, which will be the focus of this book. Be mindful, children with disability are still children. The difference between a child with or without a disability, is just that—they have a disability.

Provide them an opportunity by following the PSIA (Professional Ski Instructors of America) CAP Model[4-7, 9-11, 18,25] with age-appropriate teaching activities. Plan to adapt your lesson plan to accommodate your student's disability. Teach the movements of skiing with good judgment, especially regarding their safety.

Chapter 2
The American Teaching System

The teaching style for the disabled, is based on the American Teaching System (ATS) for disabled children. This teaching guidelines will provide consistency on how we teach throughout America. ATS is a progression oriented, outcome based and student-centered teaching blueprint.

Principles and Philosophies:

Student Centered — The lesson topics are based on the student's Disability needs.

Outcome Based — There is an outcome to every lesson.

Experiential — Individuals learn by doing it and not just by hearing, also known as learning by self-discovery.

Learning-Partnership Based — The child and instructor develop the lesson components together.

Guest-Service Driven — Students are the guests; they deserve to be taught by a specialized coach trained in this specialty.

Components:

Teaching Model

Instructor Profile — Adaptive Teaching Model

Student Profile — Background and motivation, learning preferences, attitude and other CAP issues

Alpine Skiing skills concept — edging-, pressure-, and rotary-control, plus balance

Alpine Skiing/Snowboarding Model[1]

Alpine Skiing skills concept — edging-, pressure-, and rotary-control, plus balance

Snowboarding skills concept — pivoting, pressure, tilting, twisting

Service model

Introduction — Meet and greet everyone session

Effective communication — Adapt to the student's style of talking (Pace, tone, volume, speech pattern)

A Student-Parent-Coach partnership[18, 25] must develop through constant and open communication for success to develop with your child's lessons. As the parent of your child, you need to act as your child's consultant and provide complete and transparent information to the ski instructor so he/she can know the exact and complete profile of your child to create a specific lesson plan tailored to the needs of your child. With these children with a disability, you need lots of patients and compassion. In addition, you need to always be prepared — *expect the unexpected.*

Photo 1. A thirteen-year-old girl with speech impediment is demonstrating happiness and joy because she bonded with her ski coach and developed trust. This combination allowed good connections between the student and ski instructor to deliver a memorable lesson.

A key part of your child's lesson plan will revolve around the PSIA CAP Model.[1-7, 9-11,18, 25] Every child develops at a different rate at a given age. The adaptive coach, needs to know the different developmental stages of the cognitive, motional/social, and physical developmental to create **realistic**[7,18,25] goals, and not **ideal**[7, 18, 25]goals that the child cannot achieve. A self-defeated person is always feels unsuccessful and unhappy. Be mindful that everyone wants to be acknowledged as they did a great job. The child seeks accolades so his/her parent can complement the accomplishments that were achieved. That is one of the rewards that we all seek. So, do give a lot of hi-fives on the slope. This is also a motivational factor that will stimulate the child to try harder, work harder. In this regard, whenever a coach gives feedback, it should always be *positive,* never negative because it will affect his/her self-esteem. When preparing lesson plans, use the PSIA CAP Model[1-7, 9- 11 ,18, 25] *which revolves around the child's Cognitive, Affective, and Physical developmental stages.*

3

Understanding this PSIA CAP Model[1-7, 9-11,18, 25], will aid you in recognizing the way they think, their emotion/social behaviors, and physical limits. This information will greatly help you with planning a successful lesson. The coach can adjust the lesson plans based on the information gathered and the learning style of the child with a disability:

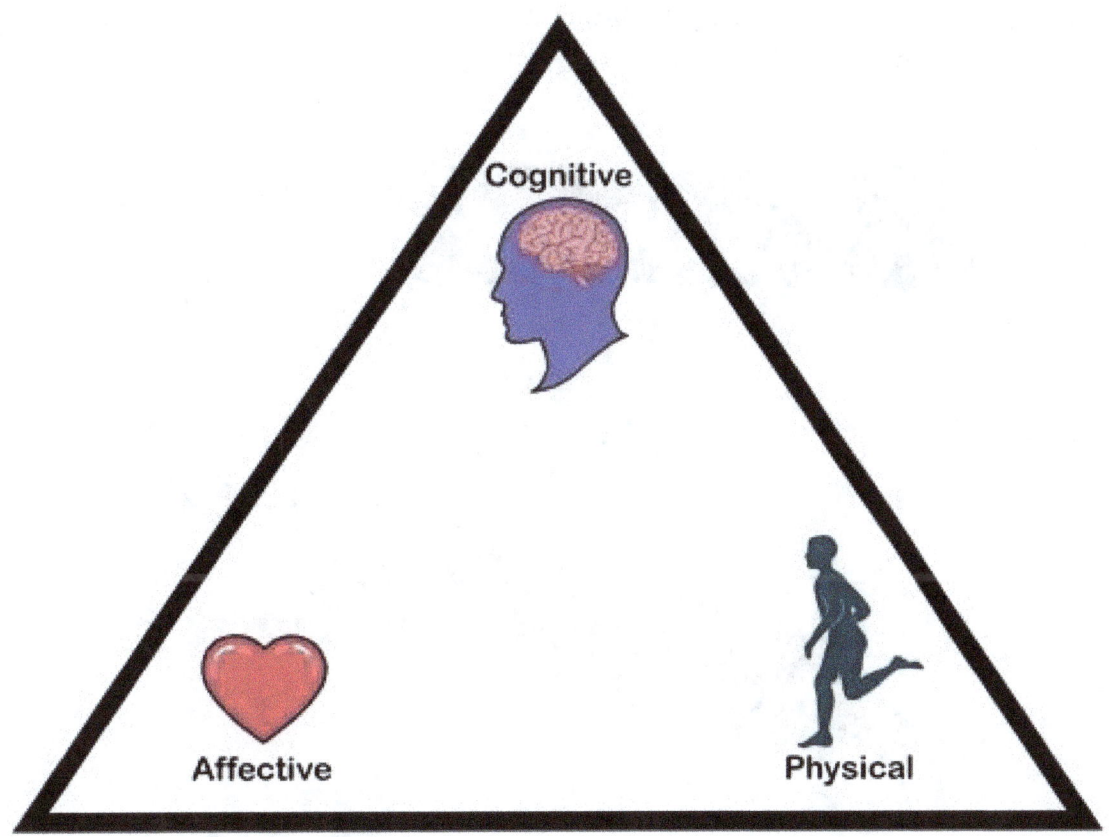

Figure 1. The PSIA CAP Model: Cognitive, Affective, and Physical Developments

Learning Styles[12, 18, 25]

People learn with different *learning styles*[12, 18, 25] According to psychologists, there are five Elements of Learning: physiological, environmental, sociological, physiological, and emotional. There are many learning styles (Verbal, visual, musical/auditory, physical/kinesthetic, combination, solitary, social, logical/mathematical).

However, it can be simplified and boiled down to the *VAK Model*[18, 25] (See figure. 2). It should be emphasized that the different styles of learning may not translate to learning the material; it simply means, according to many published reports, students prefer to receive information for processing in a specific way (e.g., Visually, or hearing the message, or feeling how to do a task).

The primary and secondary learning styles will vary, depending on the activity involved. The bottom line is, don't get too hung up on just learning styles because people learn by various methods depending on the circumstances. It is much better to think of a student having a toolbox that contains ways to think, memorize, and employ a task. However, there are many learning specialists that recommend that you hold on to a framework of the different learning styles so you can provide a rich, varied presentation when you present a new movement, activity, or skill.

Understand the *VAK Model*[18, 25] (See figure. 2) when creating your lesson plans: the three pathways by which a signal gets to the brain.

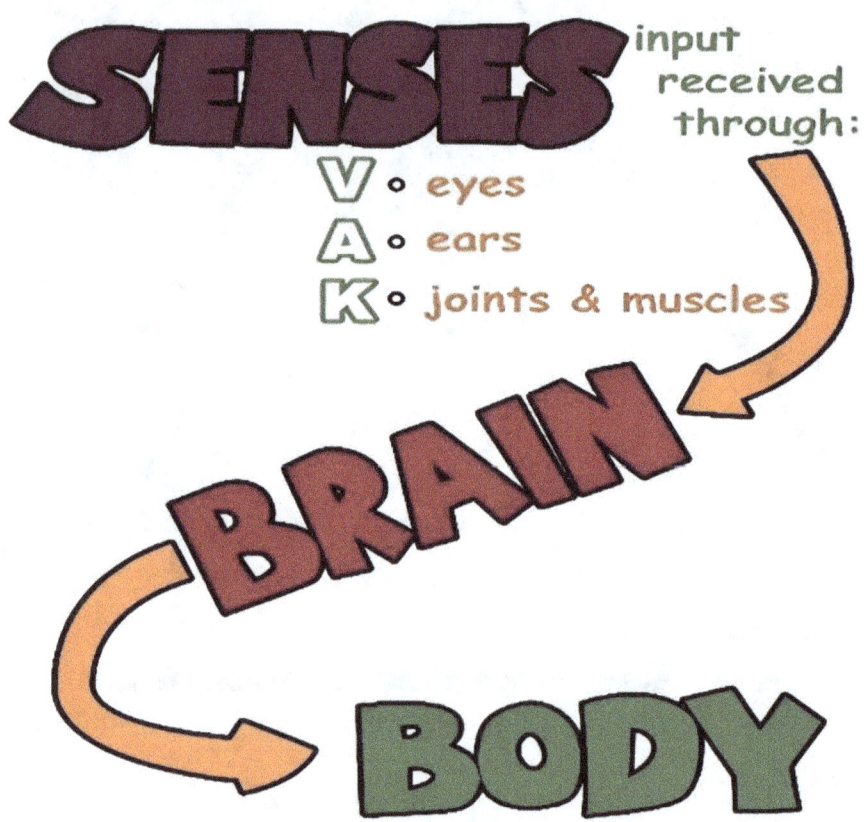

Figure 2. VAK Model: A learning style. [18, 25]

Visual

These individuals learn best when charts, graphics, images, drawings, pictures, and photographs are used instead of words. They store information in the brain as a picture and need to watch and mimic movements. They look for good demonstrations so they can copy the body movements.

Auditory

These individuals like spoken words, prefer lectures and discussions over pictures. They store information as a running commentary and need to know the *how* and *why*. These kids tend to like to listen to music, sing, and listen to the radio.

Kinesthetic

These individuals like tactile processes; they prefer to create concrete personal experiences and like to process the information by recreating and practicing. They learn best by doing activities to experience how it feels. Do ask your students, "What did you feel when doing that movement?"

With this *type of learners*, the **results** are:

I Hear, but I forget...
I See, and I remember...
I Do, and I understand...

Feeler.

These types of students need to feel the movement and activity that they are doing.

So, as a coach, you need to help them w*hat*, w*here*, *how* to feel the movements.

Remember, kinesthetic implies feeling *outside* the body; proprioceptive means feeling *within* the body.

Watcher

These types of students are visual learners and want to see how you do it (Accurate and precise demonstrations are mandatory). These visual learners target their attention to specific areas (What body parts move, how the skis respond to the movements) and prefer views from different angles. Drawing in the snow, using your hands, or using metaphors will often provide the necessary picture that they need for their brain to process. Your demonstrations need to be spot on! The same applies on what we discussed above under Visual in the VAK Model.

Thinker

These types of students ask many *how and why* questions and learn best by using cognitive abilities. They want details; so, you should provide a rational as to **why, how, when, and where** to teach a movement. They prefer a direct dialogue with you to do a verbal and/or visual discussion with them. Depending on their age, they can generally deal with abstract concepts. While keeping the instructions simple, do ask your students, "Why are we doing that drill or if I do this body movement incorrectly, what are the effects on the skis?"

Doer

These types of students want the big picture and what is necessary; they will attempt to do self-discovery on how to do it, with proper guidance from you. They will do a lot of experimentation and discover by trial and error for the desired outcome. These kids usually want to be first to go.

It should be stated that *intrinsic feedback* should be a supplement to the learning styles. Intrinsic feedback is the student's inner voice. In addition to giving extrinsic feedback, instructors need to ask students to share what they think and feel about what they are doing. For example, the student did a task and the coach said, *"Good job or that was awesome."*

The child's inner voice is saying, *"I don't understand what I just did. It doesn't feel awesome."* Intrinsic feedback is especially important to *feelers,* and for affective development of children as this becomes a reference point. In addition to giving feedback, instructors should ask the students, *"How did they feel the lesson went?"*

Remember the following:

The 3- to 6-year-old child Cognitive Development

When teaching children with a disability, don't forget they are just kids!

At this age, they do not understand concrete logic, cannot mentally manipulate information, and are unable to take the point of view of other people.

These children become increasing adept at using symbols, as evidenced by increases in playing and pretending.

They can fantasize and pretend; they truly believe that they are that person or object.

These kids are generally in their own world; they are egocentric. They can play alongside a person, but not with them.

Role-playing is important; they can act as a rabbit hopping around, be a policeman, Superwoman, a dive bomber. So, for this group, "Let's pretend" games work best.

They tend to focus only one aspect of a situation at a time (Called centration). Thus, keep instructions *simple* and *short*.

They cannot reverse the thought process, have trouble comprehending the mirror image. For example, do not face the student when doing a demonstration; instead, be next to the child so he/she can mimic your movements.

Affective Development

At this age, they are beginning to understand right from wrong.

They acknowledge adults as all-knowing and always doing the correct thing. They respect authority. They like structure and law-and-order.

Boys and girls can display a wide range of emotions.

Children who attend preschool have an added advantage over those who did not when it comes to socializing, communication, and getting along in a group setting.

Physical Development

The Center of Mass (COM) is higher because the head to body ratio is higher, which tends to put the COM behind the Base of Support (BOS).

They mature from the Top to Bottom and develop from the core of the body outward. That is why the fingers are less coordinated compared to the upper arm. The neuromuscular coordination and muscle development are less refined at the extremities.

The large muscles are preferred over the smaller muscles for skiing movements.

The 7- to 10-years old Child Cognitive Development

Their vocabulary increases to approximately two-thousand words; they can compose sentences, count to ten objects at one time.

They begin to reason, argue, and understand concepts like yesterday, today, and tomorrow.

They can copy complex shapes, such as drawing a diamond, a horse, a bird, or a snake.

The have more vivid imaginations and can act out the role more realistically.

They have a longer attention span and are willing to take on more responsibility. They can tell time, count money, know the days of the week, and can read articles of interest.

At this age, the children demonstrate more independence, self-awareness, self-confidence.

They see the world from more than one point of view.

They are very curious; They love magic tricks and ventriloquism with puppets and finger puppets.

Keep the conversation realistic; avoid abstract explanations.

Can handle more than one direction at a time, but don't overload them.

They know the difference between good and bad.

They may be able to follow a demonstration by facing them (Mirror images).

Affective Development

At this age they are somewhat innocent and trusting.

They believe in Law and Order.

At this age, they have a perspective that you are still the authority but may have little respect for your intelligence. They may challenge you with some comments that they think they know more about the topic than you do. They have the courage to question your thoughts and commands.

They are more communicative and more socially inclined to spend more time with other children.

Unlike the 3- to 6-year-old group, they are willing to share their toys and belongings with others.

They will pay more attention to friendships and teamwork. They want to be liked and accepted by their friends.

They are better at describing their feelings. They begin to feel that objects can have feelings. Their emotional swings can be greater; tempers can flair, crying can be endless, and joyous experiences can be off the charts.

They are beginning to compare themselves to other people's expectations. They love to mimic others; thus, perfect and accurate drill demonstrations of ski movements are critical.

Physical Development

The COM is slightly lower (Towards the hip) compared to the previous age group. Their motor movements are more refined, and their coordination of movements are smoother.

They can begin to coordinate one half of the body with the other half with greater ease.

Their physical strength and muscle reflexes are advancing.

Their range-of-motion with their extremities show better coordination and have and extended range as compared to the previous group.

The 11- to 18-year-old Student Cognitive Development

The students begin to verbally, mentally, and physically interact with the world around them.

The mental process is more sophisticated; logic and reasoning are more predominant in the thinking process.

With the teenagers, the information travels faster through the brain and neuromuscular system, resulting in quicker movements and better coordination.

They can process more complex problems and more abstract thinking.

At this stage they can understand the consequences of their deeds and misdeeds more clearly.

Sometimes the teens grow a bit arrogant with their newfound mental abilities. They can be difficult to deal with because they may have diverse viewpoints, believing that theirs is the most valid.

Affective Development

During the adolescence stage, peer friendship starts to become a high priority. They tend to cooperate in group settings and group games, and dislike playing alone. They spend a lot of time talking with their peers.

They develop lasting friendships and begin to deal with peer pressure.

As they mature, they demonstrate growing independence, leading to concerns with rules that can lead to bossiness.

Teen pressure plays a big role in their behavior. Good and bad are defined by the teens' social standards. Social acceptance and individual identity are high priorities.

They use problem-solving, negotiating, and compromising skills with their peers. They begin to develop sportsmanship and learn about winning and losing gracefully.

They develop a high level of competence in competitive game and team sports. They become sensitive to what others think of them; they try to seek peer approval and acceptance. Thus, do not select them to singly do a demonstration because they do not want to be judged by their peers if they do an unacceptable drill. They are very sensitive to criticisms, especially in front of their peers. Encourage activities that provide group fun, but not competition.

Physical Development

At this stage there is an increase in body strength and manual dexterity. There is improved coordination and reaction time.

There is increase in large-muscle coordination, leading to success in organized sports and games.

There is also an increase in small-muscle coordination, allowing them to learn complex craft skills. Finger and toe control are more refined.

There is increased stamina.

There is slow and steady growth with arms and legs lengthening with the hands and feet enlarging. Sometimes the periodic growth spurts can alter their coordination and athleticism, leading to awkwardness. As some parents said, "It is unbelievable that it is so common for my child to stumble over a feather at this stage of development!"

Another key ingredient needed to be a great coach is the Snow Sport Model.[15]*Safety* is the coach's highest priority, followed by *fun*, and learning, which is part of the model—use it creatively.

10

Figure 3. Snow Sports Model: Safety, Fun, Learning (Priority in that order).[12, 18, 25]

When it comes to safety, we need to be extra observant, attentive, and careful because of the limitations that these kids encounter. Some children will struggle with certain task and the coach needs to adapt to the situation. For example, the COVID-19 mask has three limitations that affect our coaching:

It limits our ability to be heard because the five layers of fabric acts like a car muffler to cut down the noise. We need to speak louder. When the snow guns are blowing and making snow, it is even a bigger challenge. Sometimes we need to pull the mask down so the student can hear us. When a child is wearing a hearing aid, be sure that the battery is working and the surrounding sound is not bothering them; many times, they will turn the volume down and they can hardly hear you.

Some of the adaptive equipment (i.e., Three-track equipment with Outrigger's sliders, sit-down ski equipment, snow bikes) are heavy and getting on the chairlift will be taxing. You may have to temporally pull your mask down and take several deep breaths of fresh air to oxygenate your lungs before continuing.

The mask will cover your smile. Children want to see your smile of approval when they do a task. Today, manufactures have been creative by making transparent plastic masks. You may want to purchase one so long as it makes a tight seal around your face.

Chapter 3
The Need to Develop Bonding and Trust

One of the primary things that a coach must do is work on developing *bonding* and *trust*[1-3,12, 18, 24] with the child with disabilities. There are several ways that the coach can accomplish this task. Besides being personable, friendly, kind, and caring, funny, I personally like doing magic tricks,[15,20] Ventriloquis[22] with puppets, or play the Harmonica[8] on the ride up on the chairlift. If you do not bond with your student, it will be an uphill battle and the learning curve will be more difficult and delayed.

Figure 4. A young boy that doesn't want to take a ski lesson and is pouting because he wasn't motivated to take a skiing lesson and is afraid to ski.

Photo 2. After a coloring book session, a ski coach reads a comic book on skiing to entertain and motivate the children with various disabilities to ski.

Have you ever noticed when you get a new pet, or a new-born baby from a relative, they seldom gravitate to you immediately? Until you spend quality time to bond and develop trust, it won't happen!

It takes kindness, loving, and enthusiastic ways.

You must show caring, gentle gestures.

Be aware that some of these children with disabilities may get colder faster You need to create fun and laughter.

You should give frequent rewards; and it needs to be reinforced frequently by verbal communications and body gestures. Notice how a dog responds to a biscuit or how a baby acts when given milk. Understand how to use Maslow's Hierarchy of Needs Theory in your lesson plans.[17, 26] (See figure 5).

Never cause harm or display disrespect for safety.

Never raise your voice or show anger.

Follow the Snow Sports Model (See figure 3): [12, 18, 25] Safety, Fun, Learning (In that priority order).

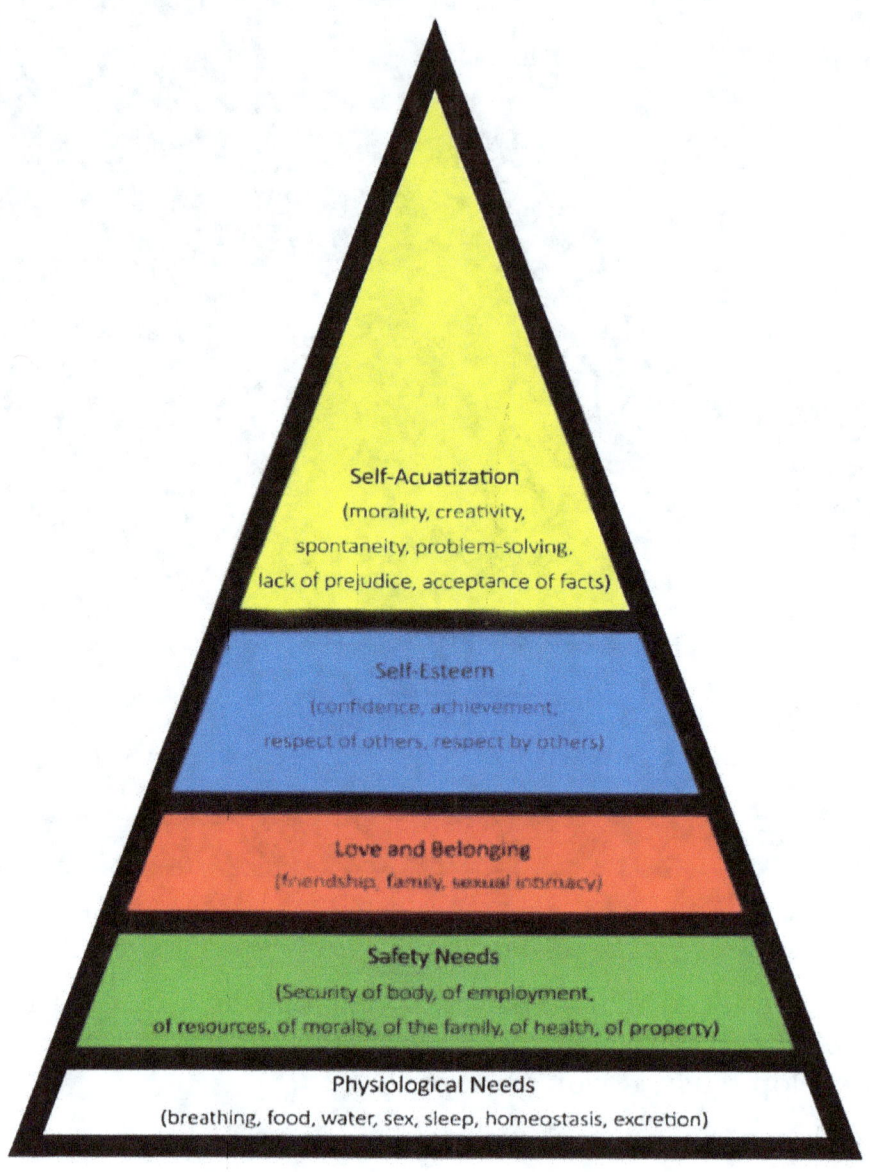

Figure 5. Maslow's Hierarchy of Needs Theory

The coach needs to unlock the student's mental attitude. To find the key to the lock, you need to discover where the key is located by asking a lot of creative questions with the student, parent, or caregiver: like what kind of sports, movies, hobbies the student likes to participate in to help understand the **Student's Profile.** Don't forget to share information about yourself to provide the **Instructor's Profile**, like what you do for work outside do for work outside of the ski school, hobbies, what you like or dislike doing for fun. Set realistic goals and keep in mind the tiny steps you must take to not overwhelm them.

It also helps to wear clean clothes, have clean smelling breath, being well groomed with a big smile, being on time for your lesson, and showing overwhelming friendliness during your introduction. It's show time! Remember, you're an entertainer to create laughter and fun.

Photo 3. You can generally tell if your child bonded with the ski instructor and learned the craft, despite having a disability, just by looking at the facial expression of the child.

Photo 4. This 3-year-old girl with a hearing issue, is expressing happiness and joy because she bonded with her ski coach through his trust, which made her lessons easier to follow and do.

Always be mindful that *Safety* is our number one priority at the ski school, your child's wellbeing is the coaches' highest priority, especially during this pandemic (See photo 4).

Photo 5. During the COVID-19 pandemic, many new rules have been implemented at all ski resorts. Here you have a seven-year-old boy with physical impairment. The wearing of face mask makes it even more difficult to hear the lessons.

Know how to Konnect© with Kids and keep **EMPATHY** in mind when you teach:

E = Eye contact; In most cases it makes better connection with the student.

M = Muscles of facial expression; Smile a lot.

P = Posture; Stand tall to show confidence.

A = Affect; Have a connection with the child to *bond* and develop *trust*.

T = Tone of voice; work on keeping it mellow and soothing.

H = Hearing the whole person; Be a good listener to fully understand your student.

Y = Your response; Be excited, be compassionate, be passionate about teaching the sport.

Be clear, open, and honest to create *bonding and trust*. For example, tell the parent and child that falling will eventually take place; but do not fret about how many times, the child fell, rather, emphasize how the child will learn to get up by themselves. One needs to be careful to not create *fear*[12] in the child, especially when they are new to the snow sport; instead, teach them to fall to the side and learn to get up. Prevent falling back (Behind the ski bindings) as much as possible, because of the possibilities to blowing out a knee ligament. Do inform them that falling is fun in the soft snow! And that you will teach them the many ways of safely getting up. You can start by practicing falling into the soft snow without the equipment, followed by falling with the skis on.

Photo 6. A young ADHD child is getting up after a fall by rolling into a prone position and pushing herself backward until she is upright.

When the child has a *meltdown*, regroup and stay close, be compassionate and stay composed. Find alternate solutions with empathy. Always keep your sense of humor and tranquility. Have patience and keep working on ways to *bond* and form a *trust*[12] with that student. In all your movement drills, always have a backup plan by using the *Stepping Stone*[7, 18, 25] teaching pathway.

A supportive learning environment starts with doing and saying things that affect trust and integrity through honesty. In addition, develop a close rapport with your kids. Make every effort to be caring, kind, loving, polite, and fun filled. Be attentive to the *tone of voice*. Behavior psychologists have noted that kids are attracted to certain of types of tones. While genetics dictate how your voice sounds, train yourself towards a more soothing and warm tone, and alert yourself to never scream or use loud tones; this is especially true with some children who have certain disorders.

Your posture reflects your attitude and confidence. Stand tall and erect when walking on the snow and kneel to make eye contact when talking to the kids. Sprinkle some humor so that you don't appear 'stiff" or 'stuffy'.

Hear the whole person out; kids want to be counted as an important individual. Don't ignore what they have to say; many times, you can pick up cues that the reason they are not listening to you or learning what you are teaching them could be something simple like having hearing problems. About fifteen percent of children have some type of hearing difficulties! Some helmet styles can also restrict sound. Solutions include speaking louder; speaking more slowly and clearly; checking if they have hearing aids and they are working properly, facing the child directly so they can read your lips, not communicating in a noisy environment, and checking if their helmet design compromises their ability to hear at normal voice levels. Your responses should always be supportive. Accept their handicaps and find a solution to make it better. Empower the child to deal with the various issues by encouraging them with positive gestures when they respond positively to your instructions. Children need reinforcement. Do things repeatedly.

I would like to share a story about developing bonding and trust that is very close to my heart. At the beginning of the ski season, I had a referral lesson from another parent. The student was a tiny five-year old girl, named Anna. She was just adorable and was cuter than a bug's ear. She had big hazel eyes and had a smile that could light up the world! During my introduction, her mom said, "*Anna was afraid of speeds and heights.*" I did explain where the parents could meet us after the lesson, and where they could watch our lesson unfold. Anna and I hopped around in the snow like crazy Jack rabbits and played green light/red light and Simon Says.

I told Anna, "*Her foot was the paint brush, and she could paint a "C" and a "J" in the snow with her right foot and then, with the left foot.*"

She learned to make a pizza with the skis off, and then with the skis on. It was time to take Anna to a three-foot runoff.

This tiny munchkin was petrified to move. I immediately knew that I had to *Bond* with her through *Trust*. I said to Anna, "*I'm going to protect you as if you were my very own child, at all times.*" I proceeded to attach the ski harness onto her waist. She went down the runoff very slowly as I regulated her speed with the harness. We continued this task for the rest of the half-hour. We worked on the gliding wedge, focusing on the athletic stance. I fine-tuned the gliding wedge by making micro adjustments (i.e., Making certain that her center- of-mass

(COM) was directly over her base-of-support (BOS). In other words, always getting her recenter on her skis for better balance. It was during that period that I began to understand her PSIA CAP Profile[1-7,9-11,18,25]: on a scale of 1 to 10 (Being the best), she had a cognitive development of 12, an affective development of 10, and a physical development of 9.5. She was an attentive and exceptional listener and executed her drills with ease.

I also asked her, *"If she would like Coco the monkey (Twelve-inch long with extralong arms with Velcro pads on the monkey's front arms to wrap around her neck) to ride on her back as we skied."* She said, *"Yes, yes!"*

I took Coco out of my backpack (Stuffed with stuffed animals, puppets, magic tricks, ski tools); she was so excited! The purpose of using the Monkey was to have her bend from the hips about 30 degrees to get her back slanted slightly into the athletic stand.

Also, I told her, *"Knees ahead of the toes; nose ahead of the toes."* I said to her that, *"if you stand upright, Coco will slide down her back, but, if she tilted her back a little forward by having her head and nose forward, Coco will be able to hang on."*

I told her that, *"That is how you need to be when in an athletic stance[18, 25]at all times when skiing."*

Psychological studies show that a person develops a liking or disliking for a person within the first fifty milliseconds to less than seven seconds. Mission was accomplished—we bonded, and trust was developed.

With the skis off, we worked on putting pressure on the inside edge of the boot and flattening the other boot while in a medium-size wedge stance. We also worked on pointing the toes in the direction of the turns (Rotary control).[25] We did the same drills with the skis on. By the end of the fifty-five-minute lesson, she was able to link the C-turns. Each step of the way, we did high-fives; I gave her verbal praises, and lots of fist bumps. I told her if she came back for another lesson, we would try a five-foot, a ten-foot, a twenty-foot runoff, but not go on the chairlift just yet, until she told me we could.

I said, *"Anna, you are the boss; I will do whatever you want."* During the second half hour, we did go higher and higher on the hill. At the end of the hour, she was making linked wedge turns! I asked Anna, *"What do you think about skiing?"* She said, *"I had so much fun, and I want to bring my best friend with me."*

Her prized reward was selecting a sticker (Butterflies) for her helmet! I gave her homework on balance by having her pretend she was a flamingo that lifted one leg while balancing on the other for five minutes every day. Her parents were tickled pink, and I was booked with her every week for the rest of the season.

On subsequent lessons, we focused on four things (1) the Skills Concept Model[24] (See page 65), (2) the Five Fundamentals of Skiing Model[25] (See page 73), (3) being balanced through the 4 phases of the turns, (See page 71), and skiing safely (See Figure 11-13, 17 and chapter 5) under speed control. By her 5th lesson, Anna progressed to being able to follow me down all the advanced slopes (Black), making beautiful, controlled parallel C-turns. Both of her parents were thrilled with her outcome, and I was invited to Anna's *sixth* birthday party at their home with her friends that summer. That's the power of bonding and trust!

When doing your lesson plans, be sure to use the PSIA CAP Model[1-7, 9-11, 18, 25] and Maslow's Hierarchy of Needs theory.[17, 26]

Figure 6. How different shaped turns affect speed control.

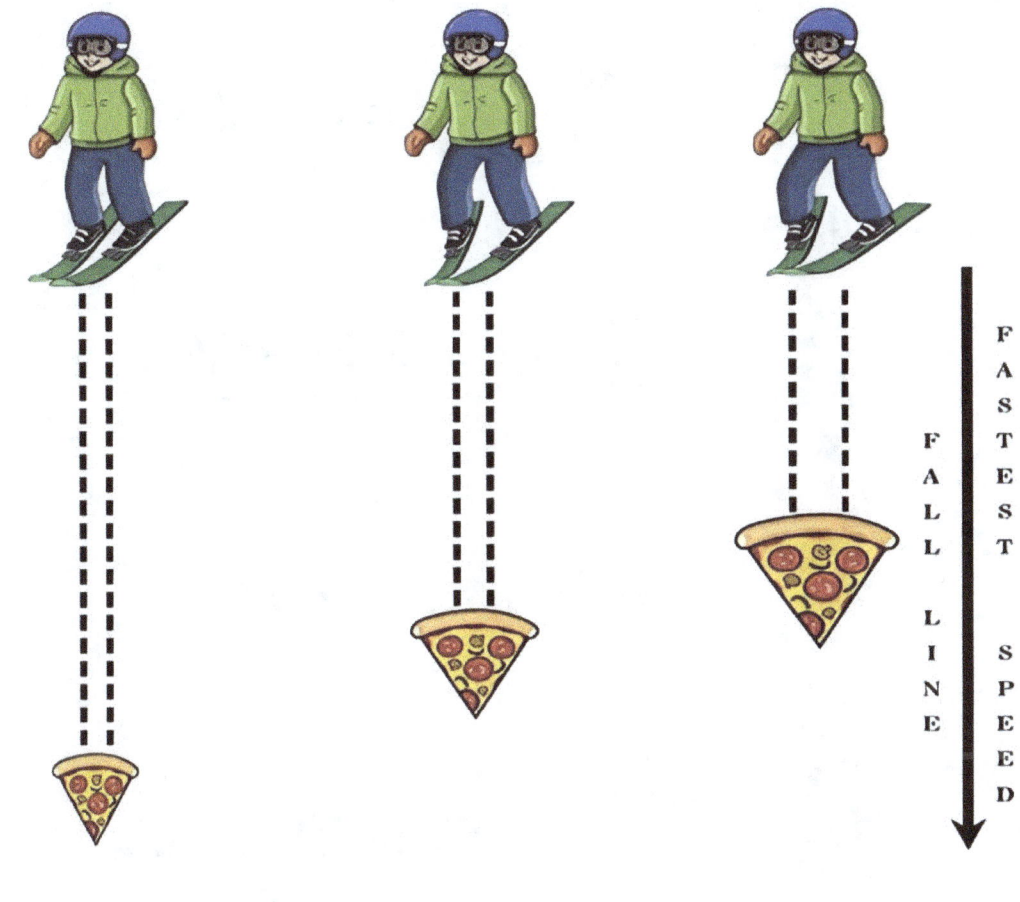

Small Pizza

(Fast, easier to turn)

Medium Pizza

(Ideal size, moderate speed)

Large Pizza

(Slow speed, harder to turn)

Figure7. How different pizzas (Wedge) affect speed control.

Figure 8. How a wedge has a different speed compared to a parallel platform.

The second story is about Memory, a three-year-old girl, who came for her first ski lesson. She and her dad were at the ski school front desk to book a lesson with me. I realized that she was afraid and did not want to go on to the snow. There also appeared to be separation anxiety involved because she had her arms wrapped tightly around her dad's leg. She squeezed his lg tight when he urged her to go out and have fun. Soon she had tears.

I told Memory that, *"I was Pineapple Herb and that I had magical powers to always keep her safe and promised her to have tons of fun on the snow."*

I did three different magical tricks (Changing the color of a handkerchief front of her very own eyes, a disappearing nickel in a tiny box, that later was found in her ski jacket (I let her keep the nickel), and a disappearing pea under one of the three walnuts that was never found) She was in awe!

To my surprise, she took my hand and we walked out to the snow without a whimper. I also asked her, *"If she would like Freddie the Frog to ride on her back as we skied?"* She said, *"Yes!"*

Boy, was she excited! The purpose of using Freddie the Frog was to entertain her on the snow and, more importantly, to have her bend from the hips to achieve a slight angle (About 30 degrees) on her back to help achieve an athletic stance[5] for better balance on the moving skis.

I told her that, *"If you stood upright, Freddie would slide down her back, But, if she tilted her back forward a little, Freddie will be able to hang on for the ride."*

I explained to the dad where we would meet after the lesson, and where he could watch our lesson unfolded. I explained to him what my goals were and **w**hat, **w**hy, **h**ow, and **w**here we would be doing her drills.

We were hoping in the snow like crazy jack rabbits. We then lifted one foot up while balancing on the other foot, pretending that were Flamingos. Next, we went sliding down the hill slowly (With a ski harness attached to her waist) with her feet making pizza of various sizes. I told Memory that, *"I'm tired of pizza, let's make French fries and go down the little hill."* At the end, I asked Memory, *"What did you think about your first ski lesson?"*

She said, *"It was a lot of fun, and that it was better than riding my bike!"* We walked in together into the lodge where I have my 12 pages of stickers and told Memory to choose one for her excellent skiing on the hill. I told Memory that, *"I was so proud of her accomplishments."* I always reward children with positive verbal comments and stickers for their efforts and successes. She picked a Unicorn Horse sticker and placed it on the front of her helmet. I was booked with Memory for the rest of the season. The point of this story is that an instructor must be creative, be able to analyze and reduce or alleviate children's anxieties and provide fun games that will promote the proper body movements to get those skis to turn in control. **FUN**[18, 24,25] is the name of the game, having the kids do fun games without them knowing that they are learning skiing movements with their bodies to get the skis to respond appropriately, is the mission of every good coach. To be successful, a coach must be creative and imaginative with the lesson plan, build bond and trust and make the student's experience fun filled and a once in a lifetime experience. Every coach should follow the **Unwritten Coach's Code** on ensuring that every child has a happy smile at the end of a fun filled lesson.

Chapter 4

Characteristics of Children with Disabilities

Collectively, these extra special group of children present a complex series of symptoms, 70 percent cognitive in origin and 30 percent physical in origin. However, as the different disorders begin to be categorized, the symptoms begin to separate based on the origin of dysfunction. There will be some overlap as we examine each disorder.

Cognitive Impairment Disorders (CID)

These are disorders[1-3, 23] which involve cognitive changes of aging and fully developed symptoms of mild-cognitive impairment (MCI), dementia, Alzheimer's disease (AD). Most degenerative conditions are characterized by insidious onset and gradually progressive decline. MCI is an intermediate state between normal cognition and dementia, which generally progresses to more serious loss of memory.

Cardiovascular disease is the second most common cause of acquired cognitive impairment. Vascular cognitive impairment includes heredity vascular dementias, post-stroke dementia, multi-infarct dementia, subcortical ischemic vascular disease and dementia, and MCI. Aging is a dominant factor in acquiring CID.

When coaching these special needs students, there are several things that the coach needs to be aware of:

Obtain a full understanding of the student's Cognitive, Affective, and Physical condition before you develop the lesson plan.

Ask the student what they want to accomplish.

Speak at a much slower pace so the special needs student can understand you.

Demonstrate your drills at a slower pace. Ask the special needs child if she/he needs to rest.

Repeat your comments and demonstrations repeatedly, and the same way each time.

Do frequent communication about the status of the individual when doing a task.

Use frequent breaks to have the disabled child repeat what he/she are learning.

Gather information from the child's feedback to see if you must revamp your lesson plans.

Have a lot of patience.

Give a lot of positive reinforcement.

Do not use the same lessons for all adaptive children, instead develop special tailored lessons for each child.

Physical Impairment Disorders (PID)

Acquired brain injuries result in many types of physical disabilities[1-3, 23] such as epilepsy, cerebral palsy, cystic fibrosis, multiple sclerosis, spina bifida, Prader-Willi Syndrome. This category of symptoms affects a person's mobility, physical capacity, stamina, or dexterity, hearing and visual impairments. These conditions usually occur after birth as a result of damage to the brain through accidents, strokes, tumors. This can include brain, or spinal cord injuries, multiple sclerosis, cerebral palsy, respiratory disorders, epilepsy, visual and hearing impairments, and more.

The physical disability can also be hereditary or congenital where the person has been born with a physical disability. Besides the loss of motor control, there is depression and loss of self-esteem.

As a coach what can you do on the ski slope? You should adhere to the following:

Obtain a full understanding of the student's condition.

Ask the student what they want to accomplish.

Be sure to use the correct ski tools to facilitate the proper movements.

Do frequent communication about the status of the individual when doing a task.

Pace your lesson at a pace that the disabled child can handle.

You may have to take frequent breaks.

Gather information from the child's feedback to see if you must revamp your lesson plans.

Give a lot of positive reinforcements.

Have a lot of patience.

Attention-deficit Disorder (ADD)

Attention-deficit Disorder[1-3,23] is a term commonly used to describe a neurological condition with symptoms of inattention, distractibility and poor working memory. This dysfunction is predominantly an inattentive syndrome.

The hallmark includes:

Poor working memory

Inattention

Distractibility

Poor executive function

This group of kids require a lot of patience and skills to control their behavior. You may want to ask their parents for suggestion on what works. Follow the KISS principle: Keep it Simple. As I often tell the coaches when I teach a clinic, *"Be Brief, be Quick, be Gone."* Stay away from loud noises like the roaring snow guns, crowds of people, children's theme parks.

Attention-Deficit Hyperactive-Disorder (ADHD)

ADD and ADHD[1-3, 23] are not the same disorder. A person with ADD often lack the hyperactivity component that is a prominent symptom with this disorder. The disorder can be neurological or psychological disorder. There are at least three major different types of ADHD. Impulsive-hyperactive ADHD, which includes forgetfulness and poor focus, organization, and listening skills.

Fidgeting

Squirming

Getting up often when seated

Running or climbing at inappropriate times

Having trouble playing quietly

Talking too much

Talking out of turn or blurting out

Interrupting

Often "on the go" as if driven by a motor

Inattentive ADHD, which includes distracted, having poor concentration and organizational skills.

Not paying attention to detail

Making careless mistakes

Failing to pay attention and keep on task

Not listening

Being unable to follow or understand instructions

Avoiding tasks, the involve effort

Being distracted

Being forgetful

Losing things that are needed to complete the task

Combined ADHD, which is the most common type; these children never seem to slow down. This includes symptoms from both Impulsive and Inattentive ADHD.

The same discussion stated for the ADD students, applies here for the ADHD children. An authoritative-management style seems to work best for this group of kids. If things really get out of hand; you may have to have a "Time Out" session. Having a bucket-load of patience will be required.

Autism-Syndrome Disorder (ASD)

Autism[1-3, 23] is a spectrum of neurological development classified as a type of developmental disability that occurs in one percent of the individuals worldwide. Everyone with autism is unique, and there is no one specific way the condition is presented. Individuals on the autistic spectrum typically experience difficulties with social communication and interaction with people. They may also exhibit restricted, repetitive patterns of behavior, interests, or activities. Symptoms are typically recognized between one- and two-years of age in boys. ASD is more than four times more common among boys than among girls. About one in six (77 percent) children (Aged 3-17 years) were diagnosed with a developmental disability during a study period of 2009-2017. These include ASD, ADD/ADHD, blindness, cerebral palsy, among others. The problem seems to be worsening. In a study with four-year-old's, ASD gradually increased between 2010 and 2014.

The term spectrum refers to the variation in the type and severity of the symptoms. Those in the mild range are typically able to function independently, with some difficulties in their daily lives. Those with moderate to severe symptoms may require more substantial support.

Long-term problems may include:

Difficulties in daily living.

Managing schedules.

Hypersensitivities to sound, light, etc.

Creating and keeping relationships.

Inducing self-injuries; a study on eight-year-old children with ASD, had 28 percent of the participants that did self-injury to themselves (Head banging, arm biting, skin scratching, hair-pulling, eye poking), making this a very common problem.

Some of the common symptoms of ASD include:

Unresponsive to others.

Minimal eye contact

Does not share interest with others

Does not pretend in play

Shows little interest in peers

Has trouble understanding other people's feelings or talking about their own feelings.

Have restricted or repetitive behaviors or interests.

Lines up toys or other objects and get upset when the order is changed.

Repeats words or phrases over and over.

Plays with toys the same way every time.

Is focused on parts of objects.

Gets upset by minor changes.

Has obsessive interests.

Must follow certain routines.

Flaps hands, rocks body, or spins self in circles.

Has unusual reactions to the way things sound, smell, taste, look or feel.

Delayed language skills.

Delayed movement skills.

Delayed cognitive or learning skills.

Hyperactive, impulsive, and/or inattentive behavior.

Unusual eating sleeping habits.

Unusual mood or emotional reactions.

Anxiety, stress, or excessive worry.

Lack of fear or more fear than expected.

Asperger's Syndrome (AS)

Asperger's syndrome[1-3,23] is a neurological disorder that is a mild form of ASD. As a (ASD)coach, you will more than likely be assigned to teach AS rather than ASD. Asperger's Syndrome is often considered a high-functioning form of ASD because children with the disorder can develop cognitive functions that match or exceed those of healthy children. However, their skills may be impaired by their ability to interact with others. A recent study demonstrated that during adolescence and young adulthood, nearly 40 percent spent little or no time with friends. Asperger's typically do not experience speech and language delays due to the above-average cognitive skills. The most common symptom is impaired social development. Children with AS focus obsessively on specific and often unusual topics. Therefore, many individuals with this disorder can become experts on certain topics. However, they have been described as socially awkward and lacking social maturity. Here are some facts about AS:

Sensory Issues

They are usually hyper-sensitive to bright light, loud noises, and certain clothing fabric. For example, a buzzing noise that goes unnoticed by other individuals may be bothersome to an AS child. Lights that are blinking, bright or flashing are common instigators. The sensation of certain fabric against their skin can be irritating and distracting, which can cause distraction.

Emotional Challenges

Children with AS may have issues with social development. For instance, they may lack empathy due to delays in social and emotional development. They may also struggle to understand nonverbal communication and nonliteral phrases, such as facial expressions. Anxiety and anger management in social situations can be a challenge for ski instructors. Many times, an AS child will express distress through emotions that do not match the situation—something that is a mild annoyance to most children can be deeply upsetting and frustrating to them.

Social Challenges

Just as with children with ASD, children with AS often prefer to play by themselves and they tend to be more self-focused. In other words, they focus more on themselves than on others in conversations and playing. Social cues such as body language and facial expression is usually missed. They can also miss the coach's hand motions (Such as 'come here', 'stop') making it seem that the child is ignoring the ski instructor or is being disobedient.

Behavior Therapies

Although AS children are different from other kids, they should not be treated all that differently. They should be praised for their good deeds and skiing accomplishments. Likewise, they should be disciplined (With the permission of the parents) like any other children and given the same structure and routine.

As a coach, what should you do? Focus on the major issues, like do not look at your student in the eye, be careful of loud sounds (Snow guns running), keep the child's drills the same; do not make changes, do not touch the student, be patient, talk to the parent on how to best deal with their child. Gather information from your astute observations to see if you must revamp your lesson plans. Keep the tasks simple and short. Set realistic goals for this ASD child. Stay calm. Always, *"Expect the Unexpected."*

Down's Syndrome (DS)

These is a genetic disorder, where there is a chromosome abnormality, that is passed on by either parent.[1-3, 23] There are over 200,000 babies born every with this disorder, causing intellectual disability, developmental delays, and physical appearance changes. The clinical features are as follows:

Eyes are shaped like almonds.

The shape of the face is flatter, especially the nose; the ears are smaller and may fold over a bit the top.

Tongue tends to stick out of their mouth.

They may have small hands, fingers, and feet.

They may have low muscle tone and strength.

They may have loose joints, making them very flexible.

They may have a short height and neck.

The head tends to be smaller.

They may have mild to moderate cognitive capacities; their ability to think, reason, understand is compromised.

Their social skills may be diminished.

Behavioral problems may exist, such as not being able to pay attention well.

They can be obsessive about some things.

They seem to have a harder time to control their impulses.

They have a harder time to manage their feelings when they get frustrated or stressed.

They are more likely to have hearing losses, visual problems, heart and endocrine issues (Especially the thyroid gland).

What can you do as a ski instructor?

Keep the teaching short and simple to minimize the frustrating circumstances or by introducing stressful tasks and drills. Follow the KISS principle.

Keep the drills the same each time you practice a given task.

Kids with this syndrome are very social and they love affection. Sometimes they will misbehave because of some underlying reason that you may have created.

Provide lots of positive reinforcements to help build their self-esteem and self-confidence. Hugs, if permitted, will go a long way.

Change your attitude and coaching approach if tasks or instructions fail; use the same ideas but modify the way you deliver the message. Rewards are important for all kids, especially special needs children. I have over three-dozen sheets of stickers that they can select from after the lesson to place on their helmet. For them it is a merit badge of honor.

Pick your battles; is the behavior dangerous or just bothersome? Avoid power struggles by giving them choices or alternative pathways to accomplish the same objectives.

Make the harder tasks and drills more fun. Make it less challenging and offer toys to have fun and take away the stigma that it is too difficult to do. With dangerous behaviors, the child needs structure and boundaries. Have 'time out' periods to cool off the behavior issues.

Be sure to communicate with the child's parents. Ask for tips on what works and don't work.

Have patients. Know your skills with these special needs children and create a lesson plan that is tailored to their special needs.

Let me share with you a story about a child with a slight disability. Lev is a seven-year-old boy who came out to ski for the first time. It was a beautiful, sunny day and I had a brief discussion with Lev and his dad to obtain goals, and developed a student-profile. The dad said that *"His son was super excited, and he talked about it for two weeks with his friends."*

When I met Lev, he didn't say much; I gathered he was a bit bashful and was on the quiet side. He was slightly tall for his age and was on the slender side. As we proceeded with the one-hour lesson; it became apparent to me that he struggled doing the side-step up the short four-foot runoff hill. I told Lev that, *"I will help him by carrying his skis up the hill and he can put the downhill ski on first while pointing perpendicular to the fall line."* We then put the uphill on, but I noticed that he could not push his boots into either binding; I had to help push each boot into each ski binding. I had to do this same procedure all lesson long. Also, he had difficulty completing his C-turns in either direction. By this time, I was able to assess Lev—his cognitive development was a 9, his affective development was a 9, and his physical development was a 6. I decided to use a ski harness to guide him down the hill as we went higher onto the slope. When we finished the lesson, I asked Lev, *"If he had fun?"* He said, *"Yeah, big time, coach!"* I asked his dad *"If there is anything I should know about your precious son?"* He said, *"Yes, I forgot to tell you that he is going to physical therapy to work on his legs, and I apologize."* I said, *"There is absolutely no problem."*

At the end of the six-week lesson, Lev was able to put his boots into the ski binding by himself and was able to make C-turns on an intermediate hill without the assistance of the ski harness!

His dad was beside himself. I have never seen so much enthusiasm and excitement among his dad, mother and Lev with his skiing performance and Lev's new love for the sport. The morale of the story is, follow the **Triple-A Rule:**

Be **A**ware

Be **A**lert

Be **A**ttentive

Visually Impaired Disorder (VID)

There are about 6.8 percent of the children younger than 18 years in the USA that have a diagnosed eye and vision disorder.[1-3, 23] Nearly three percent of children younger than 18 years are blind or visually impaired, defined as having trouble seeing even when wearing glasses or contact lenses. Here are some facts about kids with VID:

Cognitive disability had a greater influence on prevalence and kind of emotional and behavioral problems in children with visual impairment.

Social skills are compromised in children with VID.

Proprioception is compromised in the VID child; thus, space awareness around the child is an issue. Your eyes will have to be the VID child's eyes.

Lazy eye (Amblyopia) is found in two percent of young children, which makes it the most common vision loss issues. This condition is due to abnormal development of the neural connection between the brain and the eye muscles during early childhood.

The common types of VID include loss of central vision, which creates a blur or blind spot, but with intact peripheral vision, loss of peripheral vision, blurred vision, general hazed vision, extreme light sensitivity, and night blindness.

CVI or cortical/cerebral visual impairment is the leading cause of modern-day blindness in children. Retinitis Pigmentosa, Macular Degeneration and Retinopathy of Prematurity make up the four most common cause of blindness in children.

Some of the clinical signs of VID include:

Not able to see objects at a distance.

Having trouble reading.

Not able to focus on objects or follow them. They may often squint and rub their eyes a lot or have chronic eye redness or sensitivity to light.

VID students may bump into things often.

What can you do as a ski coach?

Be physically close to your student

Communicate a lot with a strong voice

Work out a safety plan that you both agree on; for example, if the adaptive student is getting close to an object, holler out, "STOP"

Your eyes will be their eyes

Know about assistive devices, technology, and other learning aids

Use ski slopes with minimal obstacles

Have a game plan to include fun games and mechanics of movements to get the skis to respond

Be sure the student is wearing a brightly-colored vest that indicates that she/he is VID or blind so the skiing public is aware; be aware some teen adaptive students may be embarrassed to wear the bright VID vest—in that case the coach should wear the vest alone to warn the skiers to keep distance from the VID skier

VID students may need a ski harness for safety

Hearing-Impaired Disorder (HID)

Hearing-impaired disorder[1-3,23] is relatively common among children. Approximately 1.9 percent of children have trouble hearing, and permanent hearing loss is found in more than 1 out of every 1000 children. Facts about HID:

Congenital, infections, physical accidents are common causes of hearing loss or impairments.

Hearing loss can be acquired through Rubella, syphilis, herpes, jaundice, toxoplasmosis, Meningitis, sepsis, certain medications (Some antibiotics, diuretics).

Head injuries, chronic middle-ear infections, some neurologic disorders (Hunter's syndrome, neurofibromatosis), exposure to high levels of noise for prolong periods.

If children do not respond to sounds, have difficulty talking, or are slow starting to talk, their hearing may be impaired.

Untreated HID can impede a child's verbal, social, and emotional development.

Hearing aids may be helpful, but today's technology still have not conquered the interference of surrounding background noise, which can be very disturbing.

HID is more common among boys.

Try to have the HID student observe your face so they can read your lips.

How to recognize HID?

Children ignore people who are talking to them—some but not all the time

Children can talk and hear well at home but not elsewhere because of the interferences from surrounding background noise.

What can you do as a ski coach?

Speak slowly and more distinctly.

Speak with greater vocal volume, short of yelling which may scare the child, or the child may think that you are trying to discipline him. Try to stand directly in front of the student so the child can read your lips.

If the child is wearing a hearing aid, check to see if there is enough charge in the battery, especially in sub-zero weather. The severe wind may interfere with hearing because the wind will force the voice away from the hearing aid and will cause distraction due to the background noise.

Try to stay away from the snow guns when they are making snow and large crowds of people.

Communicate with the child's parents to gain some tips on how to deal with their child on the ski slopes.

Speech Impairment Disorders (SID)

Speech impairment disorders[1-3,23] are disorders of speech sounds, fluency, or voice that interfere with communication. It may include articulation disorder, characterized by omissions or distortions of speech sounds, a fluency disorder, characterized by atypical flow, rhythm, and/or repetition of sounds, or voice disorder, characterized by abnormal pitch, volume, resonance, vocal quality, or duration. About 7.7 percent of USA children between ages 3-17 have a disorder related to voice, speech, language, or swallowing. Here are some facts of SID in children:

Roughly five percent of children have SID.

About three million children stutter. It affects individuals of all ages but occurs most frequently in young children between the ages of 2 and 6. This disorder occurs predominantly in boys, ranging 1.5 to 2.4 ratio boys to girls.

The types of SID include Spasmodic Dysphonia (A voice disorder caused by involuntary movements of one or more muscles of the larynx or voice box); Laryngeal Papillomatosis (Caused by tumors that grow inside the voice box, vocal cords, or the air passages leading from the noise into the lungs. It is caused by HPV virus, which is found between 60 and 80 percent in children, usually before the age of 3; cleft palate is the fourth most common birth defect, which affect 5 to 8 percent of children.

The most common SID is stuttering and lips.

A child with SID delay is likely to have difficulty following instructions, especially if the instructions are only given orally and they contain multiple words and or steps.

A student with SID may have difficulty learning how to read and spell.

What are some of the causes of SID?

Brain damage due to head trauma

Throat muscle weakness

Damage to the vocal cords

Degenerative diseases, such as Huntington's disease, Parkinson's disease, or amyotrophic lateral sclerosis

Dementia

Cancer that affected the mouth or throat

Autism

Down's syndrome

What can you do as a ski coach?

Communicate with your hands more; remember, picture is worth a thousand words; you can draw pictures in the snow.

Speak slowly and more distinctly.

You may need to speak with greater vocal volume, short of yelling which may scare the child, or the child may think that you are trying to discipline him.

Try to stand directly in front of the student so the child can read your lips.

Try to stay away from the snow guns when they are making snow. Communicate with the child's parents to gain some tips on how to deal with their child on the ski slopes.

Chapter 5
The ABC's OF SaFETY

The ABCs of Safety

The one thing that I always tell my students is that *"Speed can cause injuries. Why do you think that they have safe speed limit signs in the city and on the highway for your parents? When they exceed those safe speed limits, they can get a speeding ticket from the police, and you can get one too from the snow patrol if you don't go slow and ski safely."*

Every ski resort safety rules or codes. They may call it the Responsibility Code or some other name. I'll call it **The ABC's of Safety**.

A = Above (Always be visible to skiers *above* you.)

B = Breaks (Be sure to have the ski *breaks* working and the retention straps on your ski slopes in working condition to prevent runaway equipment.)

C = Control (Be sure you are always ski in *control.*)

D = Downhill (The *downhill* skier has the right-of-way; do not collide into them; if you are overtaking them, say out loud, "Skier on your left or right.")

E = Enter (*Enter* trails safely—whenever starting downhill or merging onto a new trail, always look uphill and yield if need to.)

F = Follow (*Follow* all posted signs; stay out of closed trails.)

G = Get (*Get* on and off the chairlifts and conveyer belts safely. Know how to Load, Ride, and Unload the chairlift and conveyer belt properly and safely.)

There are other safety issues that you must keep in mind:

Do not teach your students under the chairlifts because of the possibilities of falling equipment from above.

Do not linger at the bottom of the hill because of reckless skiers and snowboarders bombing the hill.

Do teach your students to not bomb the hill at Mach -2 speed for fear of not being able to stop when a unexpectedly change direction in front of them. About 54 percent of the deaths occurred on the blue (Intermediate) terrain; 21 percent on groomed runs; 31 percent on expert trails. Most of the accidents were males between the ages of 18 and 40.

Emphasize slowing down into the chairlift lines, instead of zooming ahead so you don't have to spend extra time and energy standing or are too lazy to shuffle ahead. You will lose only a couple of minutes! Reduce the odds of getting into an accident by avoiding the section of the hill that is crowded or congested. Skiing and snowboarding are not contact sports! There are too many preventable accidents. Teach the students to minimize distractions; sometimes listening to music or taking mobile telephone calls can increase your risk for collisions. Kids tend to play on the ride up on the chairlifts. Avoid any unnecessary movements that can cause to slide off the chairlifts; this is especially true when all the snow guns are making snow that causes the chairlift seats to have snow or ice that makes it extra slippery. About seven percent of the accidents occur on chairlifts. It is always wise to pick up the tiny tots with your ski poles wrapped in front of them and lifting your student up with hand holding each end of the ski poles. Even with preteens, I still put my ski poles across their laps, hooked onto armrest next to them to prevent any movement. This safety technique assures the student that I care about them enough, so they don't get hurt. Children are curious; make sure that they are sitting all the way back in the chair and not looking at the chairs behind them because they may twist their body and slide out. Look straight ahead and pay attention. More and more skiers are carrying a backpack filled with essentials such as water bottles, mobile phones, extra pair of goggles and gloves, radios. Inform the student to take the backpack off and place it on their lap when they ride the chairlifts. There have been reported cases of backpacks getting tangled on the back of the chairlift, resulting in accidents.

Avoid taking the student to the terrain park if you have not been trained to play in the park safely. About 27 percent of the accidents occur in the terrain parks; mostly due to freestyle skiing[19] and not following the safety rules of the terrain park.

Ensure your students are cognitively, affectively, and physically ready to challenge themselves down a steeper terrain with the proper skills to go down in control and safely, especially on the 'last run' when they are exhausted from a long ski lesson.

Never push your students beyond their mental and physical limits; this is especially true if they are exhausted, at the end of their ski lesson. Don't be afraid to call for a short 'time out' session. Many of the special needs students have clinical conditions that cause them to be fatigued quickly; do check on their status periodically. Always check periodically that *Maslow's Hierarchy of Needs*[17, 26] are being met. When a child's physiological, emotional and cognitive needs are not being met, they lose attention span.

Pay special attention to those students with physical, mental and neurological disorders or diseases and those on special medication. Watch for those special needs students that are diabetics; know the symptoms of hyper- and hypoglycemia. These symptoms react quickly (Usually within seconds or minutes), especially those on an insulin pump. I'm a diabetic myself who's on an insulin pump. I usually carry a sugar cube in my ski jacket. Check if your special needs student is carrying one too. Ideally, you should test the student's blood sugar level with a glucometer before administering any medication. The dropping blood sugar lever will result in cognition and physical imbalance. Do try to recognize the symptoms of low or high blood sugar levels.

Carry a packet of tissue, which may come in handy during the flu season or during allergy season.

Never borrow someone else's skis because the DIN setting may be wrong for those special needs child. The DIN setting is based on the child's height and weight, age, and performance level of skier.

Another safety issue can be conquering fear itself.[12]Fear can be a terrifying thing for these special needs children. It can prevent the child from trying new thing, going on a steeper terrain, and promote a tendency to lean back, resulting his/her COM to be behind the BOS. Fear can also result in the child letting out his/her emotions and refuse any more skiing instructions or may want to quit the lesson and want to go back to their parents. The coach needs to focus on what is causing the fear and try to alleviate that emotional confrontation. Work on speed control on a comfortable terrain is my first suggestion.

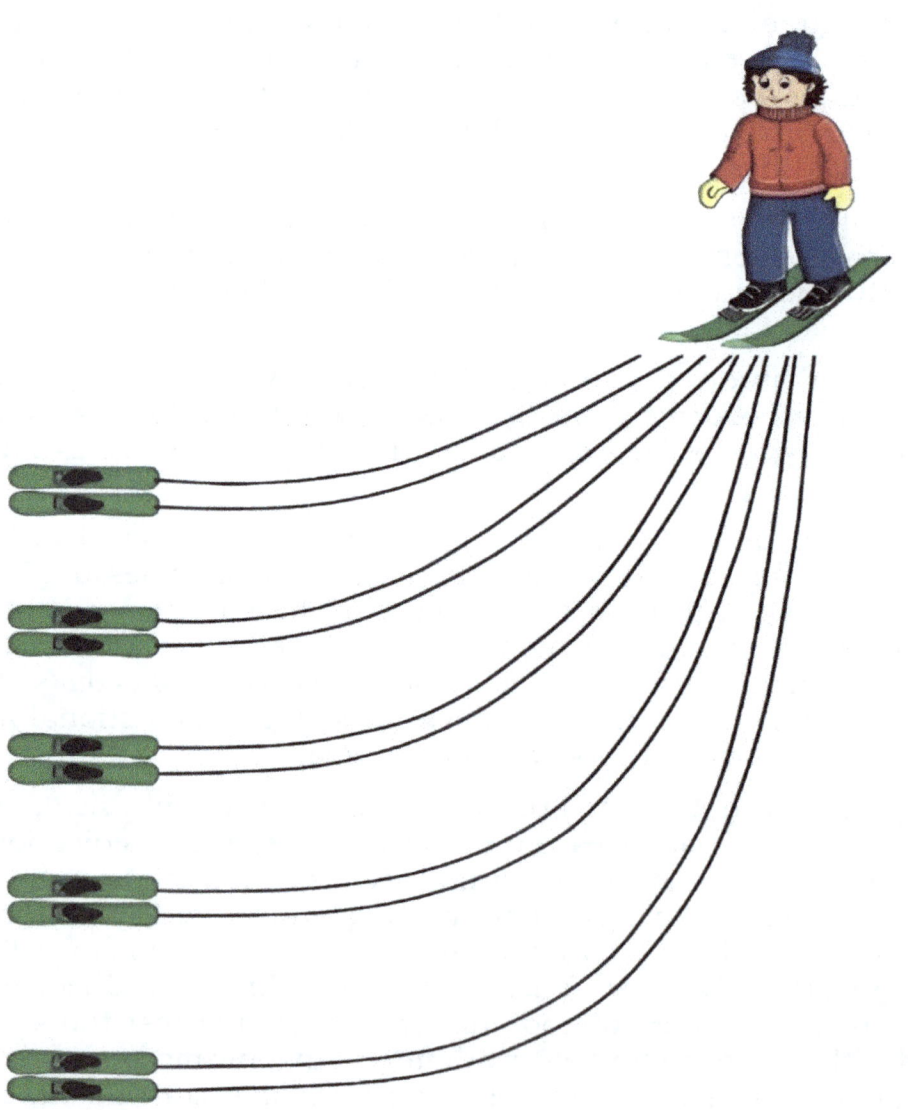

Figure 9. Fan turns: making longer and longer J-turns in the fall tine (To pick up speed) and bailing out by making the J part of "J" to finish the turn to stop.

The one thing that I always tell my students is that "speed can cause Injuries. Why do you think that they have safe speed limit signs in the city and on the highway for your parents? When they exceed those safe speed limits, they can get a speeding ticket from the police, and you can get one too from the snow patrol if you don't go slow and ski safely."

Speed control[4-7,9-11,18,24] is a high priority when it comes to the *safety* of the special needs child. You don't want to report an accident to traumatize the child, nor do you want to report the accident to the child's parents. When a child goes at speeds that are beyond his/her capabilities, they will tend to lose balance by leaning back. Here are some of the reminders that you can implement for **speed control**:

Terrain Selection

The coach should always select a terrain steepness that matches his/her capabilities. Be mindful that these special children lack many of the cognitive, affective, physical skills as compared to a student with normal skills. Always start with small steps; runoffs, then larger gentle hills, and once the different types of turns are mastered, steeper and longer runs.

Wedge Size

The coach should be able to teach the different size wedges (Pizza). While larger the wedge, the slower you go, emphasize the ideal wedge size that is hip wide. Beyond hip wide, the COM falls behind the BOS, which causes the student to be out of balance. (See figure 6).

Parallel platform

Parallel skiing affects speed control. Of the two platforms, parallel is faster than the wedge. (See figure 7).

Turn shapes

The shape of the turns also affects speed. A *J-shaped* turn allows the child to finish the turn and go uphill against gravity and comes to a stop. A *C-shaped* turn is a moderate speed turn; however, the skier needs to finish the turn to be able to control his/her speed. The *S-shaped* turns need to be reserved for the more accomplished skier because of the faster speed involved, which can create fears, and have a greater chance of being out of balance. (See figures 5-7).

Traverse

Use more of the hill so the child can have the opportunity to regulate his/her speed by heading up the hill, rather than aiming downhill and picking up speed.

Use of ski tools

The instructor should also have specialized ski tools available (e.g., A plastic hoop(s), a ski harness, poles, sleds) to help your child to control his/her speed down the hill.

Photo 7. This four-year-old girl has a rare sickle-cell disease that is found mainly in African-American people. Her anemia does not stop her from doing warm-up activities before going outside to do her ski lesson.

Photo 8. A young girl with cognitive impairment is holding on to the end of the coach's pole to assist with the turning process.

Photo 9. A ski harness is being used on this four-year-old girl with slight visual impairment to help slow her down and to assist with her turns as she weaves through the cones that simulates a racecourse.

Photo 10. The ski coach showed the children how the red ball disappeared in the red bag.

Photo 11. This ski coach is doing another magic trick; kids can NEVER get enough magic tricks at the ski school.

Photo 12. A three-year-old boy with partial visual impairment and his mom were given a complement by the ski coach for wearing a good protective helmet.

Athletic Stance

Emphasize mastering the athletic stance[5]to be in better balance to access the three skills to control their speed and turns. To stay forward and be in balance, I play a game of placing a $100 (From any game that uses play more) between the student's shin and the tongue of the boot. And I tell the student that, *"if they lean back, the $100 will fly out of the boot and they will have to owe me the money"*.

Figure 10. The student is losing the $100 bill because the girl is leaning back on her heals because she loss the shin contact with the tongue of the boots resulting being imbalanced.

Photo 13. A three-year-old girl with Autism Syndrome has her hands on her knees to assist her turning by pushing her knees in the direction of the turns.

Photo 14. A partially visually impaired eight-year-old girl is in almost perfect athletic stance while skiing on an intermediate slope. Notice that her friends are keeping a good distance from each other to prevent any accidents.

Figure 11. A stick drawing of a perfect athletic stance with the flexing of the ankles, knees, and hip, creating a 30-degree slant of the lower leg and upper torso. Note that the 30-degree slant of the upper torso is parallel to the lower leg. The yellow dots are the major body joints where flex angles are created to achieve the ideal angles to make the ideal athletic stance.

With these drills have lots of patience; be able to Adapt, Adjust, and Modify.

Riding the chairlift does cause accidents. It can happen during all three phases—Loading, Riding, and Unloading. Be extra careful and instruct the child to sit all the way back until the buttocks hit the back of the chair. In addition, I put my ski poles across the child's lap and hook the tip end of the poles onto the arm rest. here are several other conditions that require special attention with special needs children when it comes to safety:

Photo 15. When a child's buttock is below the chair, Assistance will be needed to help the child onto the chairlift, especially at higher chair speeds. Two coaches are assisting a four-year-old girl with Asperger's Syndrome safely loaded onto a chairlift for the first time.

48

Photo 16. Two coaches are safely unloading a four-year-old with Autism Syndrome Disorder safely because the off ramp is icy and steep.

One of your major goals as an adaptive coach is to get your students to make great turns using the Ski Concept Model[12, 24] and the Five Fundamentals of Skiing Model.[12, 24] Do focus on the child learning the proper ***athletic stance***[12, 23, 24.] Without the proper athletic stand, it will be difficult to implement the three skills (Edging-, Pressure-, and Rotary-controls) for excellent skiing.[12, 24]To create the correct athletic stance, flex the ankles so the knees move forward, Flex the knees so the COM move forward, flex at the hip so the torso and head moves forward, move both arms and hands forward. The angle for the tibia and back should match the 30-degree angle and be parallel to each other. Also important is where the BOS should be—hip width. Too wide a BOS will cause the COM to drop behind the BOS, leading to imbalance. For the special needs kids, I tell them, "Knees ahead of the toes, the nose ahead of the toes, and arms and hands forward."

Photo 17. A three-year-old with hearing impairment disorder and is projecting a good athletic stance. Notice: the flexing of both ankles, knees, hands, arms with the nose ahead of the toes.

Photo 18. A three-year-old boy with Mild Cognitive Impairment (MCI), mounted the People Mover safely. Notice that the ski coach behind him is waiting until there is enough distance between the two boys to avoid a collision at the top in-case there a delay in dismounting by the first student.

Be sure to spend extra amount of time perfecting their athletic stance because it is so fundamental to skiing. These special needs student need more attention and time to teach this skill. Some disorders require more time and patience.

Don't give up until they get it correct. It takes an astute eye and brain to visualize the ineffective cues to make an accurate diagnosis. Without that accurate movement analysis observation, the correct prescription to fix the problems will fail.

Photo 19. A young boy (With Type-1 diabetes) that have too wide a wedge platform, which is causing the COM to be behind the BOS; this causes her to compromise with her athletic stance.

Photo 20. These two boys with muscular dystrophy are jumping into the large plastic hoops to practice flexing and extending of the ankles and knees.

Photo 21. This three-year-old girl with thyroid dysfunction is on Synthroid therapy. She is being taught by her ski coach to do her first Gliding Wedge run on the beginner hill.

Photo 22. A three-year-old boy with Asthma is skiing out of balance. Notice: the cues[13] on the left ski is tipped onto its edge and his body is tilted to the right. This put his COM to the right of center, causing lateral imbalance.

When students are out of balance because they cannot maintain their athletic stance; one consequence is crashing. That is something you don't want because you must report the incident to the parent, the special needs child lost faith in you, and the other surrounding children may laugh at him/her. As a coach, you need to preserve the self-esteem of the individual. The special needs child may not want to try the drill again or may cry in hysterics.

Figure 12. A young child in a nasty crash because of not being able to control the speed and was out of balance.

Photo 23. A young lad with disability did not listen to his coach about the importance of skiing in an athletic stance, which resulted in a backward fall.

Photo 24. This child with a disability did not stop crying and did not want to ski any more. Using Stepping stone[11] (Plan B) did not work either. We just made 'snow angles' for the rest of her lesson time.

When the fundamentals of skiing are taught correctly, the special needs students will excel at the sport. You will have one happy special needs child and parent. Remember, your goal is to exceed customer satisfaction.[16]

Photo 25. This four-year-old boy with Type-2 diabetes is doing indoor activities to better prepare him for his ski lesson.

Photo 26. This ski coach is trying to teach this three-year-old child with Autism Spectrum to flex his ankles and knees and bend his hip to ski under the large plastic hoop.

Photo 27. A child with a rare heart disease is being assisted down the beginner slope by using a large plastic hoop to help with controlling his speed[5] while maintaining his balance and turning platform.

Photo 28. A plastic hoop is a very useful tool to help pull a child with Special Needs up the hill.

Chapter 6

The ABC's of Safety for
The Children with Disabilities

A brief description will be given of each tool as to Why, How, When, and Where we can properly utilize them to our advantage. Several photographs will be presented in this section to illustrate the usefulness of these props.

Poles

Ski-tip connectors

Ski harness

Cones and ski Brushes

Flying discs

Bridges

Horn

Poles

For a beginner, the poles are *not* recommended because of the possible distraction to the child during skiing. Also, they pose a difficulty when getting onto and off the chairlift. It is only when your child reaches toward the end of the Intermediate Performance Zone (Blue zone), that the coach will ask you to get ski poles.

Photo 29. This young lad with bone cancer is out of balance because there is unequal weight distribution over either foot or skis. Without the proper athletic stance,[12,14] the boy will have difficulties accessing the other skills.

The proper size of the ski poles should be determined by holding the ski poles upside down; then gripping just under the ski basket. It is a proper fit if the forearm is parallel to the ground.

While slightly more expensive, you may want to consider adjustable ski poles. In the long run you will save money, instead of purchasing new poles at each stage of his/her growth.

Place an address label (With a telephone number) somewhere on the poles in case they are forgotten at the ski school.

Poles can be dangerous; do inform your child to never point the basket end with the sharp tip towards anyone in front of them. It can become a weapon!

Ski poles can be useful for the instructor because they can help the special needs student control their speed and help maintain their balance when assisting them to make turns. (See Photos 30, 31, and 32 below).

Photo 30. A young girl with Visually Impaired Disorder is holding on to a ski instructor's ski pole to assist the child with controlling her speed and to maintain her balance and to assist her turns.

Photo 31. A ski coach is skiing backwards with his ski poles extended out horizontally in front of him so that his hearing-impaired student can reach out and grab the poles for speed control and turning ease.

Photo 32. A ski instructor is skiing backwards with his pole tips extended in front of him (Handle-end to the student) for assisting a teenager with osteoporosis down the hill in control.

Tip Connectors

Before a discussion is presented on these wonderful wedge-holding devices, I would like to ask the question, why teach the wedge for beginning students? Why not just teach direct-to-parallel skiing? There are three reasons why: (1) the wedge is a more stable platform for balance then parallel skiing, (2) It is a method of slowing the students down; speed is a safety issue and usually causes the child to be out of balance, (3) the mechanics that we teach for the wedge turns can be applied to parallel turns.

The ski-tip connecting tool can be used for the children of all ages who cannot make or hold a wedge. Use an appropriate length tip connector, which minimizes the chances of the tips of the skis crossing over each and cause locking of the skis. Any of these factors can compromise balance, which will affect their skiing. Using the PSIA *CAP Model*, tiny tots may not have the physical and cognitive skills to make a wedge. Neurologically and muscularly, the little ones may not have the muscle coordination and strength to make a wedge, let alone different size wedges (See figure 13 and Photo 29), Thus, this tool may help toddlers with overcoming some of their challenges (e.g., Fear of speed) by being able to execute a wedge instead of a parallel platform. There are older age children who have difficulty maintaining a wedge who need assistance.

Photo 33. A three-year-old girl with Speech Disorder is using a Ski-Tip device connector to help make and maintain a wedge platform.

Ski Harness

Ski harnesses are a great must have tool. They are a lifesaver for conquering children's fears and for controlling their speed. There are several varieties available. There are those that have a vest with a hand-lift strap high on the back and the holding straps (Reins, usually eight to twelve feet long). I do not like the ones in which the lifting handle is attached high up on the torso with the reins coming off that handle because this tends to pull the kid's upper body (COM) back behind the BOS, causing the child to be out of balance. However, that model is useful for lifting a tiny kid up on the chairlift. I suggest using those with a strap around the lower waist close to the hips with the reins (Straps) directly behind. I particularly like using this tool whenever I have doubts about a child being able to initiate a turn, shape their turn, complete a turn. or start a new turn without picking up too much speed. I even use harnesses on young adults. So, you may want several different sizes that are adjustable around the lower waist. I usually always keep the one with the smaller waist adjustment in my ski jacket pocket. I have harness large enough (Hand-made) to use with adults for this purpose. You can easily make them by cutting a ¾" or 1" PVC pipe to length and by sliding a nylon cord through the pipe and cutting it at fifteen-foot length at each end of the pipe. Use two shower curtain hangers to attach waist-width on the pipe so that you can attach a bungie-cord to wrap-around the adult customer's waist (So that the harness does not fall when you give the reins some slack).

When using the harnesses, I tell the child, *"You are the unicorn horse and I'll tug the rein on the left side several times to give you the signal to turn left, and vice versa, when I tug the rein on the right, it is the signal to turn right."* It is important to *not* always keep the reins too tight; give it enough slack to give them the freedom to ski by themselves. Only when the speed is too excessive, you can tighten up the reins to get them to regroup and get their body alignment correct to be in better balance. Many times, after several runs from top to bottom on the beginner hill with the harness, I will let go of the harness on the lower part of the slope to observe how well the child is doing the controlled wedge-turns turns down the hill. This then allows me to give accurate feedback to them immediately after the run. For example, I focus on whether they are using the child's proper body movements to get the skis to turn in link turns in control, down the slope. Use as much of the hill as possible. Be sure to check their speed using transition turns by going across the hill, side to side, rather than going straight down the hill in a narrow path. Harnesses are also useful when teaching kids to make parallel turns because the first part of the turn (Parallel skis before the fall line) can be daunting. This way, you can control the child's speed and fears when they execute the turns. What do you do with the harness reins when riding the conveyer belt or chairlift? I tuck it into their hoodie or the harness strap around their waist.

Photo 34. A ski harness is being used for a four-year-old girl with Visual-Impairment Disorder to slow her down the hill and all her weave through the cones to simulate a race course. This is one of my favorite ski tools to use for all age groups.

All too often, I see coaches *not* using harnesses and instead, substitute the harness by holding the student from the rear (By holding onto their jacket). Unfortunately, this technique tends to cause the child to instinctively lean back onto that support system and causes that child to be out of balance.

Photo 35. A three-year-old by with bipolar 1 depression is doing his first parallel run on the beginner slope.

Bridge

Skiing under a bridge is one of the favorite games among children. It can be simply made by cutting a large plastic hoop and placing each end into the snow. I like this exercise because you can coach the kids to get smaller by flexing (Closing) their ankles and then getting taller by opening the ankles (Extending) and reaching for the sky. As the saying goes, *"you always want to try and kill two birds with one stone."* With skiing under the bridge, they not only have fun, but they are working on skills that will assist with their skiing.

Photo 36. A three-year-old girl with severe hypertension is flexing her ankles and bending from her hip to get shorter as she goes "under the bridge."

Flying Disc

These flying saucers come in various sizes and shapes. They have been around for ages. Because of their light weight they can is a useful tool for teaching children. Children in beginner's lessons are generally not given poles until they are towards the end of the intermediate performance zone level, to help prevent distractions. So, what do they do with their hands?

Usually, they have their hands everywhere except up and in front of them. This is where flying discs plastic saucers can help occupy their hands and keep them in front for better balance. Dollar stores also have small plastic or rope wheels that I use because the kids can pretend that they are racecar drivers and help occupy their hands by keeping them forward.

Photo 37. A four-year-old boy recovering from respiratory-flu syndrome is being reminded to hold his arms and hands forward by holding a plastic disc (pretending to be a racecar driver), while skiing in a wedge platform.

Cones

These tools are used as markers to indicate where the directional changes should take place. Initially you could space the cones with minimal change in turn direction, and to space them far apart so that they have enough time for the child to initiate the turns and complete the turns around the cones. Be aware of the steepness of the slope when placing the cones. Speed is a detriment at this stage of their learning curve because it hinders their movements that are necessary to make linked turns. Be sure that you place the cones or ski brushes on a gentle slope so that the special needs children can manage the turns with ease.

When cones are not readily available, use your ski poles or gloves to mark the spots on the hill. You can be creative and make your own markers (e.g., Small flags, tennis balls cut in half that are brightly colored, plastic lids, ribbons tied to sticks, paint brushes (Paint the brushes with bright colors turned upside down in the snow). Ski brushes of various sizes and color can be purchased (See photo 23). Simply telling the child to turn gets boring, non-challenging, the same old

68

routine, and not fun or exciting. So, use props that they can see and interact with to have fun.

I remember, while being trained by ex-Olympians out east at a younger age, how much fun racing was. When in the starting gate, I distinctly remember how my heart raced, and how challenging it was making those turns around the gates at such high speeds on a steep terrain. In racing you do not turn freely wherever and whenever you want; your turns and turn-shape are dictated by where the gates are placed on the race hill! So, it is a more disciplined and challenging activity than just randomly turning on the slopes.

So, in your attempts to becoming an outstanding coach, build fun games, use tools that will maximize your success on the slopes and create many means of one-of-a-kind memories for the kids and parents to remember you by. For example, I like using small flags to set up a racecourse because racing uses all Five Fundamentals of Skiing.[24]

Photo 38. Ski brushes and cones are useful tools to teach different size turns as seen with this four-year-old girl who is being treated for mild depression. The girl is doing small-radius turns at the top of the hill and large-radius turns at the bottom of the hill. This simulates a race course, which kids enjoy.

Chairlift and Conveyer Belts

These devices need special attention because of the many horrific stories that we have all read in the newspapers and magazines. According to the National Ski Areas Association (NSSA), 88 percent of the accidents are on the hill, 5 percent in the terrain park, and 4 percent from falls from the chairlifts. Most of the chairlift accidents occur with ages ten and under. According to NSSA, there are 3,500 chairlifts in the USA, and 90 percent of the accidents are due to human error. Most of the lifts are either quads or triple chairlifts and riding them requires special attention.[27]

The skis and boots of a child are proportionally greater in weight as compared to the rest of the body; thus, sliding under the safety bar is more common than you think. Children are especially vulnerable when the seats are wet or icy. If you are riding up with one child, load the child on the lift operator's side in case you suddenly need help.

When you are lucky enough to have another adult to ride with you, place the child in the center, as seen in Photos 38 and 39. If you have more than one child on a triple chair, the instructor should sit in the middle and each child should sit on either side of him, all the way back and hold onto the armrest. If you have a group lesson, have a willing guest ride up with the same seating arrangement to load the rest of your class. On a quad chair, use the same arrangement; never put two kids together to fill the space because the paired kids will, without a doubt, play. For older kids, have each kid be on each end of the triple or quad chair, only if you know for certain that they are mature enough to follow instructions.

The adaptive coach should demonstrate responsible behavior, by sitting back, keeping still, having each child holding the outside handrails, and looking ahead. Instruct them to never clap their skis together to remove the snow for concerns that the skis will come off and hit someone below. I have personally witnessed a child's ski coming off and hitting someone below, causing a skull fracture.

Always be sure that the safety bar is down; if they need assistance, ask the lift operator. Another issue that needs attention is a child using their poles to load or unload, which may interfere with their partner coming on or off the lift; always instruct the student that they need to carry both poles in one hand with the pole tips high off the ground during loading and unloading of the chair. If the child does fall after unloading, educate the child to quickly get up and move out of the way for safety reasons. If they cannot get up, at least try to quickly crawl out of the way, or holler to the lift attendant at the top to stop the chairlift. When getting off the chairlift, inform your student that they need to prevent congestion in the unloading area, move away quickly so that others can come off the chair safely and go to their desired location.

Photo 39. The plastic hoops are useful for children with various cognitive, emotional, and physical disabilities to help with assisting the person by slowing down and with the turning process.

Photo 40. This three-year-old boy with recovering frostbite appears to be giving ups with his lesson.

The other consideration is demonstrating proper etiquette when standing in the lift lines. Inform your student to not let their skis move ahead and hit the person's skis in front of them. They might get annoyed because they spent a lot of money on their precious skis. As a stewardship of good moral judgment, teach your student to always have their moral compass always pointing to True North! How many times have you seen a tiny child not being able to get on or off the chairlift? It is particularly difficult when a child's buttock does not reach the chair and the chairlift hits them, and they fall; then try to get up and the child gets hit in the head by the oncoming chair. The same with unloading; when the child cannot reach the landing platform; the tiny child will attempt to jump off the chair. So, pay particular attention to a child's height relative to the chair's height. Make a sound judgement before you take the munchkins up the chairlift. With both the loading and unloading process, it is your responsibility to carry the child using whatever technique that works for you. In addition, don't be afraid to tell the lift operator to *slow down* the chairlift to assist you and the student. During the loading processes the child may need some help going from the first red line (Waiting line) to the second red line (Loading line). Inform the lift operator to please slow the chair down because it's a first timer. When the student is on the chair, be sure that the child scoots all the way to the back of the chair and hold on to the armrest. On the ride up the student should look forward and not wiggle around or play. I will usually put my arms around their shoulders and hold them for added security. If you'll need help with the unloading process, have the lift operator at the bottom to phone up to the operator at the top to *slow down* the chairlift so you can do your unloading safely. Many times, I had to get the lift operator's attention by raising both my ski poles and motion to slow down.

Horns

Believe it or not, I carry a horn with a rubber bulb in my ski jacket. I'm honking all the time when a child does a good deed or a good maneuver. It's a way to let the whole world know (Including the child's parents) that their child is doing good things. Kids love it when I'm honking coming down the hill with my student. Other children and adults find it entertaining and hilarious. See, I make everyone laugh and implant a smile on all those skiers around us. A coach needs to be extra careful when using a horn around a crowd of special needs children because the noise may create an unwanted sound and trigger an unwanted response from some of the special needs children.

Chapter 7

The Importance of the ski Concept and Five Fundamentals of Skiing Models

The Ski Concept Model[25] Edge—Control Skill[25]

Is the ability to tip the ski onto its edge and adjust the angle between the base of the ski and the snow. The edge angle can be from flat to high edge, which has a significant impact on speed and directional change. Effective edge control involves only using the amount of edge angle necessary to accurately affect the path of the ski through the arc of the turn. Skiers must move laterally to balance against the forces that act on the skis when they are tipped on edge.

There are two terms that are commonly used to describe body movements relative to edge-control skills: *angulation* and *inclination*. *Angulation* refers to movements that create angles between body parts, (e.g., Hip angulation and knee angulation).

Inclination occurs when the skier deviates from a vertical position, which is a general term for any lateral movement toward the inside of the turn brought on by the forces caused during the change in direction of the skis. Other factors that cause inclination, include the edge angle used, the size and shape of the turn radius, the pitch of the hill, snow conditions, and speed.

Pressure-Control Skill[25]

Requires body movements to manipulate forces, which affect the action of the skis on the snow. With f*ore/aft movements*, pressure can be applied to the entire length of the ski or specific parts of the ski, which requires a forward (Fore) or backward (Aft) adjustments between the skier's *Center of Mass*[25] (COM) and the child's *Base of Support*[25] (BOS). The COM is the central balance point of a person's body mass, and the BOS is where the person's weight is distributed on the foot. A skier may move the COM fore or aft relative to the BOS by flexing the ankles more (Closing), or alternately by pulling both boots back, directly under the COM. Both body movements produce the same result by adjusting the pressure fore or aft to attain better balance. The most effective way to control on the fore and aft COM is by flexing and extending the ankles. The ankles are an important part of the movements need to alter the relationship of the BOS to the COM. *I repeat, the opening and closing of the ankles can move the COM forward and backward relative to the BOS.* It is a combination of the ankles, knees, hips and upper body to are required. The fore/aft pressure along the length of the ski can be controlled by moving the COM, BOS, or the combination of both. Making minute adjustments to these body segments is hard enough as an adult, let alone as a child. Depending on where the young student falls physically in the PSIA CAP Model, these concepts may elude both physically and cognitively. The challenge is finding creative ways to get the kids to turn their skis (rotational control), tip their skis (Edging and pressure control), and direct the pressure along the ski from foot to foot. The challenge is also to manage changes in skis/snow interactions from to the bottom of the hill under different snow conditions and steepness.

Another view of pressure control is *releasing* the pressure, instead of pushing, pressing, applying, stepping, flexing, squashing. Think of it as more like *lifting*. You can lift your inside knee into your chest, to transfer weight to your outside ski. This method allows you to absorb the energy from rebound (Retraction) and project it in the direction you intend to go. While pulling the inside ski up and back, you lift the outside of the hip and lead with the inside shoulder in (Keeping the strong inside half) to execute super slow, accurate, true parallel turns. When you are comfortable with this sequence of movements, you can increase the pace. These movements are very slight, subtle, deliberate, accurate smooth, like the flow of a great gymnast. You can also lift your toes while creating a well-balanced stance on your foot to allow more closing of the ankles (Dorsal flex), if needed.

Ski-to-Ski Movements[25]

Are also necessary to control the pressure applied from ski-to-ski or foot- to-foot. During the change of direction, pressure is applied to the outside ski (Furthest away from the body's core), which causes the force to push on the skis for the change in direction. When linking the turns, the outside pressure is applied throughout the arc of the turn, and then transferred to the new outside ski for the change in direction. This fundamental concept is key to turning. You can mentally picture this by having the old outside leg flex and after finishing the turn to reduce pressure, while at the same time the new outside leg extends and lengthens. This extending of the leg increases the pressure on to the new outside ski thus, completing the transfer pressure cycle. In simple kid's terms, it's like *riding the bicycle*—long leg/short leg. It is important to know that by extending the outside leg, the COM moves *across* the BOS towards the *inside* tip of the skis and *inside* the turn. This allows the long leg to create an edge angle and pressure and the short leg to flatten the ski to allow gravity to pull the downhill ski into the turn.

Another approach you can use to teach pressure control is to flex both legs at different rates through the transition from one turn to the next. The old outside leg flexes at a faster rate than the new outside leg. With this method, the COM lowers or remains level with the ground as weight is transferred and the COM and BOS realign. This can occur in bumps and other variable terrain, and in dynamic short-radius-turn maneuvers.

Pressure Control[25]

Has a unique relationship with *balance*. The skier must maintain equilibrium to stay in dynamic balance while adding pressure to bend the skis to allow the change in direction. By adjusting the child's stance to remain in balance during turns, you need to continually adjust increase, decrease, or maintain pressure on the skis. How can you check the child's pressure control? Quite simple: I call it the *"Gloved-Hand Under the Ski-tip Test"*. Place your gloved hand under the tip region of the ski and have the student apply pressure (Closing the ankles) and check if the child needs to add more pressure onto your gloved hand by squeezing the orange that is placed between the shin and the tongue of the boot. Be aware that some special needs disorders cannot do this task. Use the stepping stone[11] pathway to create a winning task.

Rotational Control[25]

Refers to turning the skis about the vertical axis of the body. This skill highlights the ability of a skier to control the change in direction of the skis. Be aware of *leg rotation* and *counter rotation*. *Leg rotation* is defined as a movement of the lower body to affect the direction the skis point. This includes elements of rotation from the femur in the hip socket and lower-leg or below the knee (Ankle) rotation. The upper body should be the anchor (Stable point) for the rotation to be effective. For example, visualize a grandfather clock, the pendulum will not swing properly if the upper portion of the clock is unstable. Thus, keep the upper body stable so that the lower body can articulate the movements to affect the skis to change direction.

Counter rotation describes the upper body turns in one direction and the lower body (Hip and legs) turns in the opposite direction. Some call this *Anticipation*, which describes a position or anticipatory movements in preparation for turning. In this case, the upper body actively turns to face downhill rather than across the hill in the direction the skis are pointing. This process is necessary to stretch and engage muscles for the turn. Counter rotation not only provides more edge angles but assists with the turning because the lower body is 'twisted' from the upper body and the lower body wants to unwind to a neutral position. The upper-body rotation alone is typically an inefficient movement. The proper sequence is as follows: the upper body turns first, followed by the legs turning in the same direction as the lower body unwinds. The separation of the upper body and lower body will assist in the turns. Inexperienced skiers tend to use the whole upper body twisting technique to get the lower body to turn via the inertia of the upper body. Children do this because they do not have the proper body developments or use inappropriate movements (Because of the lack of knowledge) to initiate the turn, (e.g., The child will use the child's only upper body to "swing" into the turn). As a coach, you should be aware that depending on the age of the child, they have not developed the upper- and lower-body separation and are more "one-body" in their rotational movements. Why? Because their neuro-musculature development dictates that type of movement. So, for the time being, focus on the lower body by getting the skis to point in the direction of the turns (Rotational skills) until the child has more cognitive and physical developments.

When skiing parallel, both corresponding edges are released simultaneously as both skis are tipped into the turn. The BOS needs to stay under the COS; this is done by pulling the skis slightly back and manage the rebound energy through retraction. When the COS is aligned properly over the BOS, you are in much better dynamic balance. Most of the skiers push the skis slightly forward at the end of a turn; you have just lost balance and power by not being able to flex the ankles enough to pressure the edges. Another issue that contributes to ineffective turn initiation is skiers lack the patience to let the ski seek the fall line; instead, most skiers push the skis (Heels) laterally to get the skis out of the fall line as quickly as possible, thus, interrupting the ability to shape the turn. Great skiers possess the ability to shape turns in the control phase and are so refined that they can adjust the arc of the turn while they are in it by employing *DIRT* (**D**uration, **I**ntensity, **R**ate, and **T**iming) of the skills applied during the turn.

Balance[25]

Is fundamental to good skiing. What is Balance? Simply put, it is the body's attempt to maintain equilibrium in basically an upright position by conscious and non-conscious (Automatic) reflexes. There are four key body parts that are involved in balance: three sensory organs (Eyes, inner ear, and proprioceptors), and the brain where incoming information from the three sensors is forwarded to the processing and control center, which is the brain. Proprioception is the body's sense of self-movement and body position. These highly specialized sensory organs send messages to the brain about the limb's velocity and movements, the amount of load on a limb, and the limb limits. These complex series of neuromuscular networks account for knowing where our body parts are in the environment, and to help maintain a desired position. See photograph 5 showing a young child on the balance beam. Knowing this, what can you do to improve the child's balance? Study fig.

8 carefully for a good athletic stance.[12, 24] Practice, practice, practice the right fundamental movements. All athletes practice fundamental movements intensely with the guidance of a skilled coach. My golf coach once told me, *"Practice is useless if you don't practice the proper skills and mechanics of the golf swing. If you don't, when you go to the practice range, all that you will do is just reinforce bad habits"*.

Other Considerations on Balance

A common debate is whether being in a state of dynamic balance creates the ability to move more effectively by using the other three skills, or vice versa. The answer for this dual role of balance is "yes." In addition, you need to recognize the interdependent relationship between the skills and balance, the results of effective and efficient movements. Since most of your students are out of balance (Usually in the 'back seat' of the middle of the skis), focus your attention on this movement skill. When I communicate to a child, I ask the child, "When your parents drive the car are they in the front seat or back seat?" Invariably the answer is, "In the front seat." Then, I tell them, "Well, you're driving those skis, you'd better be in the front seat of your skis!" "If you are not in the front seat, you will lose control and the skis will run away." The size of a younger child's head is larger in proportion to their body. When coupled with growing motor-skill developments, the aforementioned can change the balance points.

Because PSIA and AASI have made gradual modifications over the years by NOT considering *balance* as a skill, but rather an outcome of developing the blended elements (Skills) of the edge control, pressure control, and rotary control, do examine how we use these elements *in The Five Fundamentals of Skiing* throughout the text.

Photo 41. This girl has a Speech Impediment Disorder; rather than be teased she decided to take sign language class to avoid the harassment.

Photo 42. This teenage boy with ADHD was going at a high speed on the hill. You can tell by doing Movement Analysis: the right ski is convex shaped rather than concave shaped. The skier is tilted forward.

How can we translate the physiological definition of balance into a practical and realistic definition? Since most of the instructor's focus in working on balance during various activities, let's break the movements down into segments. In this discussion I will utilize the *Five Fundamentals of Skiing*[46] (Which is discussed extensively in the next section in this chapter) to illustrate the movements necessary for turning. In a static exercise, balance begins with the upper torso, head, arms and hands (Called the center of mass, *COM*) are centered directly over the foot (Called the base of support, *BOS*) so that there is equal pressure on the entire foot, from the toes to the heels.

In an **Athletic Stance**,[12, 25] the body is in a readiness position. Here, the COM moves slightly forward by flexing (Closing) the ankles so that the knees move forward along with the COM and the pressure on the foot moves to the center of the arch of the feet, and sometimes towards to the ball of the foot, depending on how aggressive one is skiing and other conditions.

Since we spend most of our time teaching turning maneuvers of different shapes, size, and speed, let us focus on *balance* as we go through the different phases of the turn.

Four Phases of the Turn

There are *four phases of the Turn*: (1) Phase 0 or *Transition Phase,* which is not usually mentioned in the PSIA manual, (2) Phase 1 or *Turn Initiation,* (3)

Phase 2 or *Shaping of the Turn*, and (4) Phase 3 or *Finishing of the Turn. See Photos.*

Photo 43. A thee-year-old girl with Type 2 diabetes in a good athletic stance [5] Note: her ankles are flexed to move the COM forward to be centered on her feet (BOS).[24]

Photo 44. A young girl with Type 2 diabetes too wide a wedge, which causes her to sit back (COM falls behind the BOS); this results her to compromise her athletic stance[24] and be out of balance. Too wide the wedge (Opposing edges) the more edge angle it creates the slower you go, but the child will be out of balance because the COM will be behind the BOS.

Photo 45. After each ski lesson an evaluation is made on the child's performance. Here an anxious mother is being informed about her child's performance.

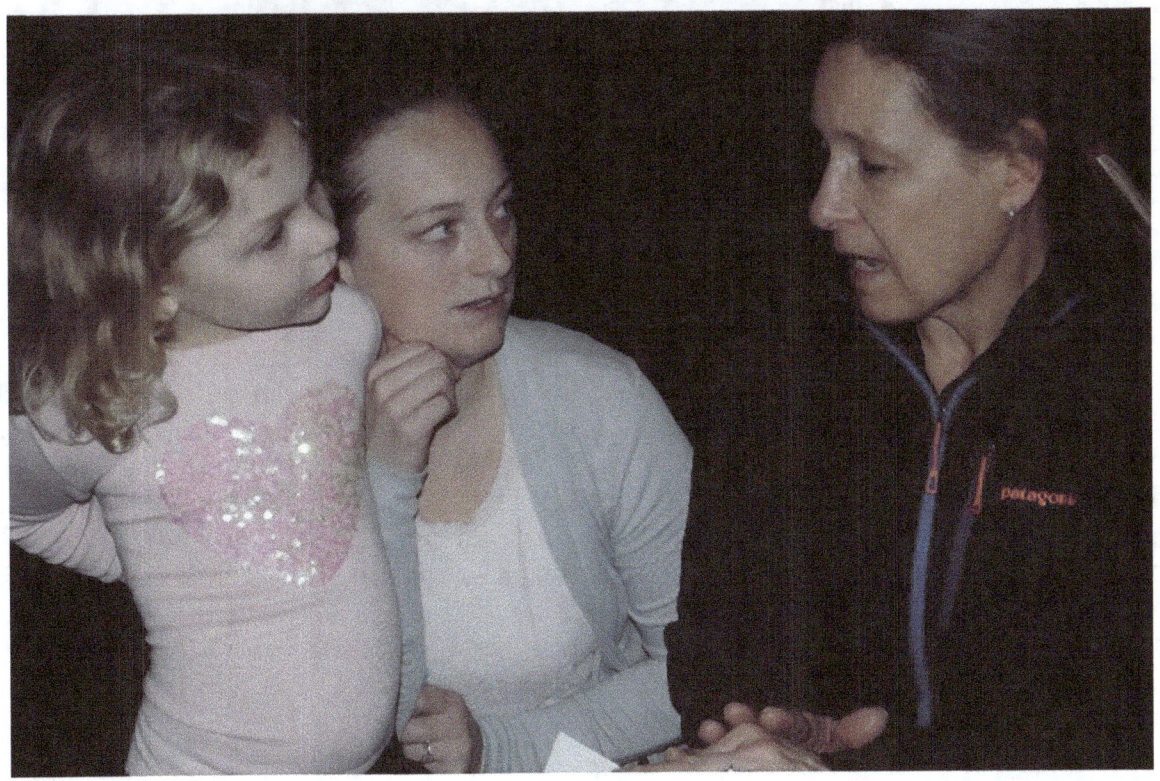

Photo 46. Another ski instructor is informing a parent how her little girl performed during her ski lesson on wedge turns.

Photo 47. Indoor foot drills: this three-year-old boy with hearing-impairment disorder is doing ankle drills.

Transition Phase

While this is an often-neglected discussion, this is an important phase of the turn. Many skiers are out of balance as they finish a turn and enter this regrouping (Transition) phase. If one is out of alignment and balance, there are couple of things that one can accomplish to re-center the COM over the BOS during this phase. One is flexing (Closing) the ankles to get the COM over the BOS, and second to pull both feet (BOS) back under the COM. Most skiers tend to rush going from one turn to the next without giving themselves enough time to regroup. One of the drills that I have the students do is the *2-4-2* concept. Provide enough time when the student has 2 edges on the snow to allow time to get back into balance with 4 edges on the snow, so that one can begin the turn initiation more effectively with 1 edge engaged from both skis.

Turn Initiation

The beginner skier in the wedge platform can begin to initiate the turn by moving the COM diagonally towards the inside (Downhill) skis tip. This causes

83

the outside (Uphill) leg to lengthen and the inside (Downhill) leg to actively retract—like pedaling the bicycle (e.g., Push down on one pedal as the other pedal moves up) or doing heavy foot/light foot drill. The skis will react by the outside ski having more edge angle and pressure to initiate a change in direction of the ski. The inside leg is actively shortened and is thereby closer to the center of the body with little or no edge angle (Almost flattened on the snow). This causes the ski to release the contralateral edge to disengage from the snow and allow gravity to pull the inside tip downhill as the uphill or outside ski follows. The movements for the parallel skier follow the same sequence of events except that both corresponding edges engage the snow at relatively the same time and causes both skis to change direction in unison. With both the wedge and parallel skier the rotary skill is also used to blend with the edging and pressure skill to start the turn. It is key to remember that weight transfer shifts from a neutral position to the outside ski and one should be balanced throughout the turn on that one ski.

Shaping of the Turn

This is the fastest phase of the turn because of the amount of time that is spent in the fall line. The greatest speed and force occur at the apex of the arc. The speed is determined by the turn shape (See figure 6) and by the size of the wedge (See figure 7). The shape, size and speed of the turn is determined by *DIRT*. Don't neglect the affects of the wedge versus parallel platform (10).

Photo 48. Ski Kids Programs always have balloons
of various sorts to add entertainment for the children.

Photo 49. There can NEVER be enough balloons when there are children around the ski school.

Finishing the Turn

The major objective of the finishing phase of the turn is to control one's speed. Many students do not finish their turns and they tend to pick up too much speed and get out of balance and control. Coaches should emphasize the importance of this phase of the turn.

Photo 50. A ten-year-old boy, with upper-respiratory disorder drops his arms, hands, and poles after finishing a turn. This causes him to be out of balance because his COM is now behind his BOS[25].

Five Fundamentals of Skiing Model [25]

This section will provide you with a short overview of this important model. Additional readings are provided in the references.

Direct Pressure to the outside ski and pressure control from ski-to-ski: Transferring your weight to the outside or inside ski and being balanced is not an easy feat. After finishing a turn, it is a fundamental goal to get balanced over the downhill or outside ski or balanced over the uphill or inside ski. When making a right turn, it is a left-footed turn, and when making a left turn, it is a right-footed turn. Pressure increase/decrease can be achieved couple of ways; one of which is by lengthening the leg, or by shortening the leg. The ankles (Opening and closing) and the knees both play a major role in extension and flexing motion. Retraction of the legs is another way for adjusting the pressure on the skis. Do not neglect the proper position of the hips relative to the BOS when focusing on balance. Drills that can be utilized for this fundamental skill is discussed further in chapter 6.

Photo 51. A twelve-year-old boy is using the Five Fundamentals of Skiing[24] when making a left turn by having the right ski on edge by extending the right leg (Long leg) and having the left ski flattening out by retracting the left leg (Short leg). Also, the weight transfer is on the outside ski.

Photo 52. Even a 4-year-old girl can make great turns using the Five Fundamentals of Skiing[24] if the ski instructor coached a student correctly.

Control Edge Angles with Inclination and Angulation[25]

Tipping the skis onto their edges, involves inclining the body toward the inside of the turn in the direction you are turning; it also involves angulating the upper body back toward the skis (Toward the outside of the turn). When making a right turn, move the uphill hip and shoulder up; keep the downhill hip and shoulder down. The opposite movements are done with a left turn. The COS needs to move in the direction of the turn. As discussed in the Skill Concept Model, edging can be achieved through inclination, angulation, or both. The foot or ankle articulation also plays a role in edging. Drills for this fundamental skill is discussed further in chapter 7).

Keeping the COM over the BOS[25]

Controlling the COM to stay over the BOS is always a challenge during any type of skiing. Staying in balance to utilize the entire length of the skis, the front of the skis and the back of the skis when need, is a tough fundamental to master. The results of this control are better stability and balance; and better control on how the skis turn. Staying in balance in the center of the skis is your primary goal. See drills in chapters 6 and 9 for more edging activities. This concept of attaining *dynamic balance* is covered extensively throughout this manual.

Photo 53. Whenever a person rides a People Mover or a chairlift, advised them to view and appreciate the beautiful scenery that nature provided.

Figure 13. Flamingo Drill: A great drill for practicing balance by lifting one leg and balancing on the other. Make it fun by timing yourself as to which leg is more coordinated and stronger.

Controlling the Skis' Rotation[25]

This can be achieved by (Turning, pivoting, steering) with leg rotation that is separate from the upper body. The upper body (Core) should be quiet and stable, while the lower body rotates independently by twisting the femur (Upper leg) in the hip socket to the right or to the left. More is covered above in the *Skills Concept Model* section under "Rotational Control." (See Chapter 6).

Regulate the Magnitude of Pressure Created through Ski/Snow Interactions[25]

You can create resistance by pushing down on the snow. The force a ski puts into the snow acts at a right angle to its surface. The reaction force also acts at a right angle to the base of the ski. There are two things that you can do with a ski which will affect the reaction force and its components. The first is to tilt a ski onto its edge, and the second is to change the angle that a ski is pointing in along its length. As a ski's resistance comes from the ski's reaction from the snow, two forces can push the ski into the snow, gravity, and a momentum-induced force from changing your velocity. Gravity always acts straight downwards with a set force. The momentum-induced force will only act if you are changing velocity; this creates a G-force as we turn. This is a difficult topic to understand, but whenever you go out skiing, focus on these forces that create pressure. Try to determine how the pressure skills are interwoven into the *Five Fundamentals of Skiing Model.*[25]

When contemplating an activity, ask these questions of yourself:

What movement pattern will we be practicing?

Why are we going to perform this activity?

How will it enhance my lesson and affect our skiing today?

Where are we going to do the drills?

Chapter 8
Games to Create Fun and Learning for Adaptive Children

The name of the game is to develop creative coaching and make your lessons exciting and fun. There are hundreds of ways to do that, and I am certain you can add to this list of adventures, drills, and games[1-7, 9-11, 18, 24,25] Whenever you introduce fun games, bear in mind that they should involve one of the skills. Be mindful that not all children can do all these drills based on the PSIA CAP development; so, modify accordingly. Since kids love to mimic what you do, make certain that your demonstrations are *spot on.*[5] I will list them by categories of primary skills involved. Depending on what performance zone the child may be in, do not expect that he/she can do all the specific drills listed; you need to use proper judgement. Many categories of listed activities overlap one another:

Edge Control[25]

Boot arcs — Draw smiley faces and Sad faces in the snow with their boots.

Duck walk — With the ski tips pointing outward and having contralateral edge pressure, the skis can grip the snow to move forward like in the herringbone walk.

Gloved-hand under the ski-tip test — This is an excellent way of determining how much edge pressure is being applied to the front of the ski by your student.

Side stepping — Using corresponding edges, do side steps up the hill.

Outrigger Turns — This is a great edging and pressure drill. This drill emphases the need to get the legs as far away from the body to get more edge angle. As the child is traversing the hill and is balanced on the inside (Downhill) ski, extend the outside (Uphill) ski as far ways from the body as possible and apply ample pressure to start the turning process. Continue applying the correct amount of pressure throughout the turn do get the desired turn shape and size.

Cowboy Turns — One-legged and two-legged turns; this is a great edging and pressure drill (It is discussed in greater detail in chapter 9, under "Advanced Zone").

Feeler Turns — This is a great drill to keep the upper body quiet, while using the ankles, knees, and hips to articulate the turns with edge and pressure controls. (This drill is discussed in greater detail in chapter 9, under "Advanced Zone").

Hockey stops — For some reason the children in the intermate and advanced zones love this drill; it involves more counter movement for greater edging and pressure control with rotary control.

Side slipping — This is a great drill for edging and pressure control for the parallel skier; the corresponding edges should increase the edge angle and pressure to stop, and release when you wish to slide down the hill. Lateral balance is also involved with this drill.

Skiing the side wall of a hill — This is a great game and drill to break the habit of a wedge and moving on to parallel skiing by racing to the top of the sidewall. One can only get to the top, if the skis are in parallel and not in a wedge position.

Big toe turns — Getting inside edge and pressure by squashing the bug with the big toe.

Pinky-toe turns — Getting the outside edge and pressure by tipping the pinky toes.

Playing the piano with both toes — This is a great drill for changing directions with linked-parallel-turns; combine both the big-toe turn and pinky-toe turn simultaneously.

Squashing the marshmallow with the big or little toes and the arches of the feet —This is a great homework and on-snow drill for edge and pressure control; place a marshmallow under the arches of a barefoot or pretend under the center of the boot and push down with a pronation pressure.

Double-fisted Turns — This is a great edging and pressure drill; and for the ankle and knees to move together the same amount, side-to-side; this is especially useful for women who are knock-kneed.

Upper/lower body separation — Great for creating more edge angle.

Scooter turns with the other feet off the snow — Since you can only ride one scooter at a time, for each turn to the right and to the left, you need to hop on the scooter (Weight transfer) and moves the knees and feet in the direction of the turns. While being balanced on the scooter tip the big toe and pinky toe on edge. (See Photo 54).

Long-leg/Short-leg Turns — This is a great drill for flexing and extension as well as for all four skills.

Pressure control[25]

Grabbing for the stars — Great flexing/extension drill; extend and reach with both hands and pluck the stars out of the sky; and come down by flexing and bending the knees to put them in your front pockets. Shooting the basketball into the hoop — Great flexing/extension drill; extend and jump shoot the basketball with both hands and come back down and dribble the ball, by flexing your ankle, knees, hips.

Heavy foot/Light foot: Great pressure drill; one foot is forcibly placed on the snow (Ski) and the other foot (Ski) is raised slightly off the ground. This drill can be extended to include elephant walks, bicycle ride, long-leg/short-leg exercises.

Picking apples and putting them in the basket — With both hands forward in an athletic stand, the downhill hand reaches for an apple and plucks it out of the tree and places it in the basket strapped to the downhill boot — All the while skiing in balance.

Squashing the bug — A fun drill for edge and pressure control; place the insect under the big toes and bury it deep into the snow! The exterminator has now eliminated all those nasty bugs!

Popcorn — A fun drill for flexing/extension static or dynamic exercise; pop, pop, pop—throwing your hands up in the air and hopping each time the corn kernel pops).

Walking on Hot Rocks or Hot Sand — A fun exercise for flexing/extension drill; ouch, ouch; the rocks/sand is hot, and it is burning my bare feet—we're hopping around like crazy people.

Hopping like a Jack Rabbit — A fun flexing/extension activity like the popcorn and walking on hot rocks/sand drills.

Pedaling the bicycle: like the popcorn, elephant walks, hot rocks/sand, riding the bicycle are great weight transfer and pressure and balance drills. There are so many skills that are included with peddling the bike.

Car shock absorbers — Great retraction exercise; ride over small bumps making the sure that the child's head is touching the ceiling all-the-while the legs are retracting (To absorb the bump) and extending (When it finishes the bump). If the shock absorbers do not work, your head will go crashing through the ceiling!

Jumping rope — Another good flexing/extension activity like the popcorn and walking on hot rocks/sand drill.

Gloved-hand Under the Ski-Tip Test — I mention this exercise again because it has helped me so much. This is an excellent way to evaluate how much edge pressure is being applied by your student. This is discussed in greater detail in the Ski Tip on the Gloved Hand test.

Rotary control[25]

Wedge Christies — This is a great drill for balancing on the downhill ski, while using rotary on the uphill ski. Try doing wedge christies while doing garlands; it becomes a real challenge; I think it is an underutilize drill for the older children.

Garlands — Great drill for weight transfer and rotary, edging and pressure control. You can continue with the wedge christie exercises and fuse it into garlands.

Making bowties or hourglass figures — Great static rotary drill, focusing on rotary leg movements with a pivot point under the arches of each foot; if there is too much snow to do this drill, place the ski pole on the ground and place the center of the boot over the handle end of the pole and make bowties and hourglass figures with greater ease.

Windshield wipers — Another great static drill for rotary. Be sure that the leg should be rotating all the up into the hip socket, Also, be sure the pivot point is not the heels, but, instead, from the arch of the foot.

Pizza/French fries — This exercise on rotary movements is a favorite for children. This drill needs careful attention; be sure that the movements have leg rotation all the way up into the hip socket and pivot point is under the arch. All too often, I observe coaches telling the student that to make a pizza from a French fry, byo kicking the hills out while keeping the ski tips together; WRONG!

Fan progression turns: Great for increasing speeds as the fan turns get progressively longer. The increasing speeds require more force to rotate the skis on edge to make a J-turn. It is also my favorite exercise for conquering fear by making progressive longer J-turns while in the fall line and bailing out when the speed exceeds their comfort zone.

Wedge changeups — This drill requires changing from a pizza to French fries, and vice versa. This is a great rotary drill, like the pizza and French fry movements. Careful attention is needed to be sure where the movements are originating from. Is it from the arch of the foot?

Gliding wedge — Your primary focus should be on whether the COM is over the BOS to be in an athletic stance while in a wedge platform gliding down the hill.

Headlight turns in the dark — This is a fun drill. We are going to be looking for frogs in the dark. The headlights are the palms of their hands, which need to be up and facing in the direction of the turns. Keeping the hands up and forward (Pointing in the direction of the turns) also causes a slight counter movement for easier turning because twisting movement causes the skis to want to return to their natural position because of the unwinding process of the counter rotation. Pointing the toes in the direction of the turns also helps.

Pointing the toes in the direction of the turns — This is another version of twisting the feet into the direction of the turn. There's a little ankle rotation going on, but the major turning process is from the femur rotating in the hip socket.

Balance[25]

Athletic stance[5] — This is a body's position with a hip-wide foot stance, a flexing of the ankles to get the knees forward, a bending of the knees to get the hips forward over the center of the feet, with a spine angle of approximately thirty degrees from the hip, and with the head and eyes looking straight ahead. The arms should also be forward. (See figure 8 in chapter 3 and Photo 20 of a three-y-old girl with good balance mechanics. Also examine children in good balance (Photos 13, 14, 17, 2527, 30-32, 34-38, 43, 51, 52, 58, 61, 62, 64, 68, 70, 71, 76, 79, 82) and in poor balance (Photos 18-24, 28, 34, 40-42, 44, 47, 50).

Pedal the canoe — In the athletic stance, reach forward towards the tip of the ski, and pedal back to slightly behind the ski breaks, while maintaining balance.

Hop Turns — This activity was discussed in the "All four Skills" section.

Shuffle Turns — This activity was discussed in the All four Skills section.

Riding the scooter — This is a great drill for weight transfer and balance. When you ride the scooter, the weight is shifted to the foot on the scooter and balance is maintained onto that same foot. (See photo 54).

Flamingo, crane, stork with one leg up — This is a fun balancing drill on snow or for indoors (For homework).

Thumpers — While balancing on the downhill ski, thump with the uphill ski as one traverses the slope; and reverse the drill by being balanced on the uphill ski and thumping on the downhill ski while traversing the hill.

Tap dancing — This is like the Thumper drill; just sing a bit...and tap, tap, tap.

One-thousand steps — Like this drill, because the 1000 steps are a great drill to check if your body alignment is correct, especially when going through the turns. There should only be a smooth, continuous turn without hesitations. If hesitations occur, then the student is out of balance and is regrouping his COM to be over the child's BOS during the hesitation.

Fly like Superman or Superwoman — With hands forward, check the child's athletic stance while skiing.

Driving a race car — Like Superman or Superwoman drills, keeping the hands forward with a steering wheel, help promote proper balance.

Spearing the frog — Spearing a frog ahead of you or to the side of you require fore or lateral balance. Do not use this exercise while demonstrating pole touch. By stabbing the frog or salmon, causes a delay in removing the ski pole tip from the snow and causes the downhill shoulder to open, causing the skier to be out of balance.

Keeping a $100 dollar bill between the shin and tongue of the boot — This a great exercise to promote shin-tongue always contact (See figure 9).

Touch and turn — Pole touches are a timing device to gain rhythmic turns, a reminder to turn around the pole, creating a stable upper body with a triangular support with both legs and planted pole in the snow.

Knees ahead of the toes — This is done by flexing the ankles to get the COM forward over the BOS. Sometimes, children have difficulties doing this movement for two reasons: (1) they don't have the strength to do it, and (2) the plastic shell is too hard to bend for this age or skill level. When buying boots for your child always check to see if the plastic shell is soft enough to bend the boot.

Nose ahead the toes — Same with knees ahead of the toes; it allows the knees, hips, and upper body to move forward. One of the things that I do is to tell the kids, "If you don't want blood from a nosebleed to drip onto your beautiful ski jacket, be sure that your nose is ahead of your toes. I also tell them your nose won't grow like Pinocchio's to stick out over your toes; the only way is by bending at your hips. Try it!"

Holding the tea serving tray — This exercise keeps the hands forward and during the turns causes a counter movement because the tray needs to be facing the Queen of England, who is sitting in her throne at the bottom of the hill. Also, tell the students that the tray needs to be level; do not spill the tea!

Butterfly wings — Flapping the wings of a butterfly promotes fore/aft and lateral balance. Girls seem to love this activity.

Airplane wings of a dive bomber — Tipping the wings into the turns cause the uphill hip, shoulders and arms to tilt upwards, while the downhill hip, shoulders, and arms will tilt downwards, causing a better body alignment with the terrain for turns. Boys love this activity.

Jumps — Like hoping, it is a great flexing/extension exercise for pressure and balance control. (See Photos 20 and 54). We use this activity indoors a lot with markers on the floor for balance and pressure-control (By flexing, extension of the ankles, knees, hip, and pressure).

Clapping their hands in front and back while skiing — This is great static and dynamic drill for promoting balance; more advanced skiers can use a pole to pass from the front to the back while skiing.

Jumping — This is an excellent drill for practicing flexing and extending the ankles for pressure skills.

Balancing board — Anyone serious about improving their balance, can purchase any type of board with a hard ball or tube underneath to challenge your balancing skills.

Photo 54. A three-year-old boy with ADHD likes jumping on the markers that are placed on the snow to practice flexing and extending the ankles, knees, and hip for pressure control[18, 25].

All Skills with Balance[25]

Red light/green light — You can even add yellow light. Kids really enjoy this game. They will engage in this activity until the cows come home. What's nice about this activity, it involves all the skills and balance.

Ski like an animal — This is fun activity because we do heavy elephant walks around the children's theme park (Primarily rotational- and pressure-control with balance), swimming like a fish for making many turns (Primarily rotational skill and balance), walking penguin (For weight-to-weight transfer, pressure control, and balance) flamingo standing on one leg (For fore/aft and lateral balance).

Hand skiing — This activity is used a lot when using a face mask for airborne virus protection. Visualization of what the skis are doing (e.g., Tipping, edging) is helpful for visual learners and when you can't be heard because of the face mask or when all the snow-making guns are running.

Follow the leader — This is a fun game. The students have their own ideas as to what is fun. Generally, all the skills and balance will be used.

Spreading the peanut butter and jelly — Inform the students they need to use their skis to smear the snow. (Edge and pressure control).

Cat and mouse — This is a fun chasing one another game that uses all three skills and balance.

Traffic cop or ski patrol — Like the cat and mouse game, it is a fun chasing one another game that uses all three skills and balance.

Simon says — Kids love playing this fun game, which uses all 3 skills and balance.

Synchro turns — This sophisticated game is for older children who have intermediate and advanced performance skills. The turns will take a lot of timing, coordination, and synchronizing of the eyes and body to match everyone's turns. To make things easier, I shout out turn, so everyone turns at the same time.

S-Turns: These turns are for faster speed while making turns down the hill. I focus on the turns being the same size (About a fifteen to twenty feet corridor width.

C-Turns — This is the "bread and butter turn" for medium-controlled speed down the slope. I focus on the child finishing the turn to help keep the speed constant.

J-Turns — As mentioned before, this is a great turn shape for making a turn and coming to a stop. Blend this turn into the progressive fan turns to help alleviate fear of speeds.

Falling leaf — Like side slipping, it is a great drill for edging- and pressure-controls; it also utilizes lateral and fore/aft balance and a little bit of rotary-control when pretending to be a leaf falling to the ground.

Pivot slip[25] — This is a great drill for advanced skiers. It is a useful maneuver to learn because it can come in handy when going down a narrow corridor. It uses all Five Fundamental Skills of Skiing. Before you execute this activity, check the snow conditions and texture. A hardpack snow is more suitable than soft snow, ice, or ice chunks called "cookies".

Scavenger or treasure hunt — I hide treasures purchased from the dollar store and hide them on the hill for entertainment, this game uses of all skills and balance. I provide a treasure-hunt map to inform the students where the golden nuggets are located on the hill.

Hockey stops — This maneuver should be reserved for intermediate and advanced level students. I focus on when and how they make the 180 degree turns and come to a stop with their ski edges. Key to this maneuver is to keep the upper body facing directly downhill. Some children will favor a right turn or a left turn.

Skating: if you make this into a competitive race by placing two ski poles ten feet apart, they will have a blast. I will first demonstrate the movements that are necessary to do perfect skating. This is one drill that I especially like because it uses all three skills and balance, and it can be useful when going from point "A" to point "B". This activity should be reserved for those students that are parallel skiing.

Cones for Racecourse — There is no doubt Kids of all ages love racing. It certainly beats just making turns on the slopes. It appears that the more advanced the children's skills are, the more they like the sport. It's a fun activity and uses all three skills and balance.

Racing — On certain days of the week, we set up a full racecourse. We need to have attendants at the starting gate and the finish line to ensure safety. Whenever a student crashes in mid-course, we stop the next child in the starting gate. This activity is fun and uses the Five Fundamental Skills of skiing.[24]

Hop Turns — This is a fun activity that uses flexing and extending of the ankles, knees to make the hops, using pressure- and rotation- control into the turns while maintaining balance.

Shuffle turns — This is a great exercise for intermediate- and advanced performance-level students. This is an excellent drill to check on proper alignment of the COS over the BOS throughout the turn. Like the 1000step drill, if there are hesitation doing this exercise, it reflects the child is out of balance.

Throughout the text I have shown many photographs that displayed many fun drills for children with various types of disabilities. I have gathered other fun drills and exercises for you to examine below:

Photo 55. A child with disabilities is being assisted down the beginner's hill by using a plastic hoop to help with speed control[18, 25] and to assist the student to help maintain balance while turning.

Photo 56. When I have extra time between lessons, I will try to have a snowball fight (After getting permission from the parents). If the special needs student is not wearing a helmet and ski goggles, I will aim below the chin for safety reasons.

Photo 57. This young lad was not too happy with the outcome of this snowball fight. In fact, he was whimpering just beneath his breath. **NEVER** *intentionally throw a snowball directly at a student's face!*

Photo 58. Hurrah she did it! A three-year-old girl with recovering COVID-19 variant infection is doing her first Gliding Wedge run on the beginning hill.

Photo 59. This three-year-old girl with an emotional disorder is crying during her ski lesson because she did not bond with her NEW ski instructor.

Photo 60. This coach is pretending to be a reindeer to entertain the children on the beginner hill. He created a lot of smiling children!

Photo 61. A four-year-old girl with ADD is scooting on her 'scooter' to practice weight transfer and pressure control while maintaining balance.

Photo 62. A three-year-old girl with a physical disability is flexing her ankles, knees, and hip to get shorter without losing her balance as she goes under the "London Bridge."

*Photo 63. Kids, who have an Adaptive Disorder
are doing indoor drills to enhance their skiing skills.*

Photo 64. A three-year-old girl with upper gastro-intestinal problems is doing her first gliding wedge run on the beginner hill.

Photo 65. Many times, riding the chairlift to the top of the hill makes it difficult for the special needs child to go down the hill safely. The ski instructor should use a carpet that goes 10' to 25' up the hill to assist the student. If you need more flexibility, use 2' x 2' squares to adjust the desirable length you need. The student should be able to do the side-step or herringbone walk up the carpet.

Photo 66. A four-year-old boy with Type 2 diabetes is being assisted by his ski coach to learn the side-step movement on a homemade wooden ramp for easier drills as compared to the outside snow.

Photo 67. A shy four-year-old girl practicing her herringbone walk on flatland before attempting to climb the hill. To climb the hill, she will be encouraged to make bigger ice cream cones (Wider ski tips) to create more edge angle for better traction.

Photo 68. This teenage girl is using the Five Fundamentals of Skiing to carve around the giant slalom gates.

Photo 69. This lucky three-tracker is experiencing total bliss because he is not only skiing through a ton of trees, but also through deep, fluffy powder.

Photo 70. This four-year-old totally blind girl is being assisted by her adaptive coach to do a wedge turn. The visually impaired skier needs a lot of room. Some special needs skiers are totally blind, and they need a wide birth, because they only respond to the coach's vocal directions, which might result in a delayed action. The coach needs to be the student's pair of eyes.

Photo 71. *This partially blind eleven-year-old girl is being instructed verbally by her ski instructor.*

Photo 72. *When teaching a blind student, be sure to outfit the special needs individual with a bright-colored vest that indicates that the skier is blind to inform the public to ski around the person with caution.*

Photo 73. Mono-skier requires balance and strength. It also takes more time to learn. It is less stable compared to bi-skiing with handheld or fixed outriggers.

Photo 74. Bi-skier with handheld outriggers have a more stable platform as compared to mono-skiing. From a sitting position, they should be able to push up with their arms until their arms are straight and hold that position. The adaptive skier should know how to get up independently after a fall.

Photo 75. A two-track skier distributes his/her weight equally on both skis. The upper body remains quiet and disciplined and the pressure-control movements are minimal. Vision stays forward, in the intended direction of travel.

Photo 76. This teenage girl with speech-impairment challenges is trying her best to carve around the giant slalom gates by using the Five Fundamentals of Skiing.[25]

Photo 78. This amputee has a prosthesis. This skier may or may not need a sit-down adaptive equipment, depending on his/her cognitive and physical abilities.

Photo 79. A four-track skier using a sit-down adaptive ski chair.

Photo 80. The ski instructor is telling the student with muscular dystrophy to bend her knees to form an athletic stand.

Photo 81. This teenage adaptive student could not physically finish her C-turns and loss speed control. Fortunately, there was a safety net to catch her from plowing into the brick house.

Photo 82. A seven-year-old boy with a physical disability is small jumps in the terrain park with good skiing fundamentals.[25]

Photo 83. Children prefer boots feeling like bedroom slippers, instead of feeling like a firm handshake. This three-year-old girl is in boots that is slightly too large—you think!

Chapter 9

The Importance of
Teaching the ABC of Safety

It is estimated that over six-hundred-thousand injuries are reported each year nationally, as a result of skiing and snowboarding. Make sure that you fully understand your ski resort's safety policy. Indicate how you intend to implement this into your lesson plans. Later, at the closing, explain to the parent and child how and where you taught *safety*.

Every ski resort has their version of the Responsibility Code[1-5, 12-14,18,25] I'll call this The ABCs of Safety:

A = Above (Always be visible to skiers *above* you).

B = Breaks (Be sure to have *ski brakes* working and retention strap on your skis poles to prevent runaway equipment).

C = Control (Be sure you always ski in control).

D = Downhill (The *downhill* skier has the right-of-way; do not collide into them, If you are going to overtake them, say out loud, "S*kier on your left or right.*").

E = Enter (*Enter* trails safely—whenever starting downhill or merging on a new trail, always *look uphill* and yield).

F = Follow (*Follow* all *posted signs*, stay off *closed trails*).

G = Get (*Get* on and off the chairlifts safely. Know how to load, ride and unload the *chair and conveyer belt* properly and safely[18,25]).

Other Safety Guidelines:

There are *other safety issues* that need special attention with COVID 19. With the viral air-born pandemic, the ski industry is going through a major revolution for safety.[14] In conjunction with the National Ski Areas Association (NSAA) and PSIA/AASI encourages everyone to follow the national guidelines, "Ski Well, Be Well" (nsaa.org@skiwellbewell). Review periodic guidelines for safety updates that are aligned with the Centers for Disease Control (tiny.cc@COVID-19 CDCGuidelines.com).

This is your responsibility! All ski resorts all over the world are struggling to maintain the pandemic safety and have posted many rules for protection: this has been a year of experimentation for survival.[2] There are other ways that you can help protect yourself from this virus[39] besides social distancing, wearing a facial mask or balaclava, and sanitizing your hands and ski gloves often. There is absolutely no doubt that wearing a mask and social distancing is a worthy protection during the lesson.[14] You can also eat healthier meals, improve the quality of your sleep, avoid tobacco, drink less alcohol, minimize stress, increase your physical activity, improve your gut health with probiotics, and increase vitamins A, B-6, C, D, E, zinc, selenium, iron, folic acid.

I have discovered that there are at least three compromises when you are coaching and wearing a mask. (1) You will have difficulty communicating; your students: they cannot hear you are saying, and you cannot hear them. The mask will act like a car muffler to reduce the engine noise. So, at the very beginning of the lesson, you need to carefully explain that you will try to speak *louder* and more *clearly*, if they cannot hear you, inform them that they should say, "Please repeat that, coach."

[3]You may want to step back and temporarily pull your mask away from your lip and let the volume of air and sound out to more readily reach your emotions besides jumping down, clapping your hands, doing other body movements to show signs of approval, excitement, and acceptance. Since every child seeks a beautiful smile of approval, you may want to student(s). The student can do the same thing so that you can also hear them. I can't imagine the struggles that we will go through when all the snow guns are making snow! (2) It will be extremely difficult to show temporarily lower the mask to show your smile. Today there are creative manufacturers that are making face masks that are made of clear plastic so people can see your facial expressions. (3) When you are skiing hard and seem to be out of breath, try lowering the mask and take two to three minutes of deep breathing to reoxygenate your lungs.

Other safety issue include:

- Do not coach your students under the chairlifts because of the possibilities of falling ski equipment (Poles, skiis).
- Coach them to not bomb the hill at Mach-2 speeds for fear of not being able to stop when a person unexpectantly changes direction in front of them. About 54% of the deaths occurred on blue (Intermediate), groomed runs; 31% were bon Expert trails. Most of the accidents were males between the ages of 18 and 40.
- Use a larger wedge size to slow down into the lift line, instead of zooming ahead, so you do not have to spend extra time and energy standing in line or are too lazy to shuffle ahead.
- Reduce the odds of getting into an accident by avoiding the section of the hill that is crowded or congested. Skiing and snowboarding are not contact sports; however, people do collide into one another. Minimize distractions; sometimes listening to music or having earbuds to take a mobile phone call can increase your risk for collisions.
- Kids tend to play on the ride up on the chair. Avoid any unnecessary movements that can cause a student to slide off the chair; this is especially true when all the snow guns are making snow and the chair has snow on it and it freezes, making it extra slippery.

It is always wise to pick up the tiny tots with your poles wrapped in front of them, lifting your student up with both hands holding each end of the poles. Hold them in tightly next to you. Even with teenagers, I still put my poles across their laps, hooked onto the arm rest next to them to prevent any movement. And this safety technique assures them that I care about them enough about not getting them hurt. Children at this age are curious; make sure that the students do not try to see what is happening on the hill or chair behind them because they may twist out of the chair and fall; this important safety topic was discussed in greater detail in this chapter, under the topic, "Chairlift." It is becoming increasing popular to carry a backpack, containing essentials such as water bottles, snacks, extra pair of goggles, cell phones, radios. When riding the chairlifts, take the backpack off and place it in your lap. There have been reported cases of backpacks getting tangled on the back of the chairlift resulting in accidents. Avoid taking them into the terrain park if you have not been trained to play in the park safely. About 27% of the accidents occur in the terrain park, mostly due to freestyle skiing.

- Ensure your students are cognitively, affectively, and physically ready to challenge themselves down a steeper terrain with the proper skills to go down in control and safely, especially on the 'last run' when they are exhausted from a long ski lesson.
- Never push your students beyond their mental and physical limits; this is especially true if they are tired or exhausted, at the end of the lesson. Don't be afraid for a short 'time out' even though the time of the lesson is not over.
- Always check periodically that Maslow's Hierarchy of Needs,[17,27]especially the physiological and safety needs are not being met; the child can be easily distracted and not obey what is being told when they have higher physiological or mental needs.

Diabetes[29]

Diabete[29] in children with disability is not normally covered in adaptive kids skiing handbooks. However, it is a common disorder with 210 ,000 individuals under 20 years of age diagnosed with Type 2 diabetes annually, and steadily rising each year. A common cause is being overweight. Obesity in the USA is overwhelming, involving about 14.4 million children and adolescents (About 20 percent of the population) who will eventually become a diabetes candidate. This is a high-risk factor for developing diabetes as they get older. Because of these statistics, I decided to briefly mention this endocrine disorder. Pay special attention to the special needs individuals that need more attention, besides those with certain physical, mental, neurological disorders, and those that are on special medications.

Do ask the parent, "Has your child been properly fed? Has she/he received their daily medications before going out on the slopes?

Also, being a diabetic myself, I always keep sufficient rapidly-sugar cubes in my pocket if my blood sugar level plummets. Some diabetic children keep sugar tabs or candy in their pockets in the event hypoglycemia (Low blood sugar) occurs. Ideally, before taking any sugar product, testing the sugar level with a glucometer is recommended. The dropping blood sugar can result in the loss of cognition very rapidly (Usually within a few minutes). Do try to recognize the symptoms of low sugar in the blood (Hypoglycemia):

Loss of cognitive function resulting in dizziness, confusion, comma, or even death

Irritability

Jittery

Loss of attention to what is being taught

Sweaty

Thirsty

Too much exogenous insulin or diabetic medications can result in the blood sugar to rapidly plummet, (i.e., Usually within a few seconds to a few minutes).

What can you do?

Recognize the hypoglycemic symptoms.

Stop what you are doing and immediately take the child to the parent or the Ski Patrol hut.

Provide sugar if you are *certain* that it is a hypoglycemic reaction and not a hyperglycemic reaction.

Ask the parent if there are anything special that you should know about Johnny. If he is a diabetic, ask if he had a good meal before of the lesson, if he took his diabetic medications, did he recently test his blood sugar?

The symptoms of high blood sugar (Hyperglycemia) are similar to hypoglycemia. While both conditions are important to recognize, hypoglycemia is the more important one to focus on the hill. A person's blood sugar level is affected by three things: Medication, Diet, and Physical activity (See figure 15). Any one of those triad will affect the sugar level. Thus, you have a challenge on the hill. You can ask the child:

When did you last eat?

What did you eat?

Did you take your medications?

Are you carrying a glucometer?

The blood sugar status of the child is dependent on:

The amount and kind of diabetes medications taken.

The amount, the kind, and timing of the food intake.

The duration, intensity, and frequency of the physical activity (See figure 13) and the amount of insulin or other glucose-lowering medication taken. Any time the child shifts one of the components in the triangle, i.e., increasing the amount of physical activity (Like skiing) or not eating the usual diet, the sugar metabolism will be out of control, resulting in the symptoms described above. Certainly, inform the parents of this incident.

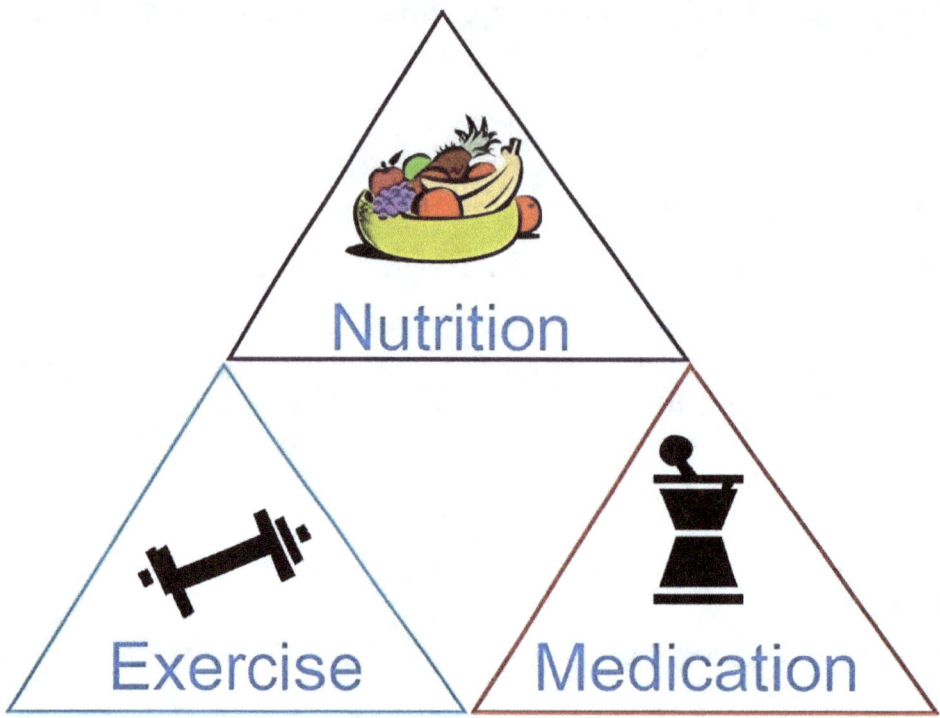

Figure 14. Diabetes Triad[29]

I also recommend carrying a small pack of tissue in your pocket in the event a tiny tot needs any assistance with a runny nose. Wintertime is flu season so, also keep a small bottle of hand sanitizer handy, especially in this era of new airborne viruses. Frequent disinfecting the hands *and* gloves will be the new norm for the future. Little things like this can avoid distractions and can lead to a better outcome of a critical and challenging situation:

Teach the children how to carry their skis properly when walking to and from the ski lodge. As this is a high-traffic area, be especially careful when changing direction so that you do not hit someone else.

Never borrow someone else's skis; the DIN setting may not be correct for their height, weight, age, and performance level skier.

Another safety issue can be conquering *fear* itself.[16] Fear can be a terrifying thing, preventing a person from trying something new, or sitting back (The COM is behind the BOS), or letting emotions get out of hand and the child refuses any more instructions or wants to go back to their parents. Fear can, sometimes, be good, promoting caution in dangerous circumstances, like a steeper slope or going into the terrain park. There are some kids that have no fear, and they can be a real hazard on the hill. As we get older, we file more fear factors and experiences into our brain. Some of the files are overfilled! You can keep the student on a lower terrain doing different drills to hone in their skills. Eventually, that same terrain will become boring. Now, the challenge sets in on introducing the new steeper terrain. On a less-steeper terrain, you may want to try the fan turns. Tell the student that going straight down the fall-line (With the speed increasing may be too much), they can bail out and make a J- turn. To put it another way, as the straight runs get longer, the speed enhances, but they can always bail out and do a J-Turn. When the student understands there is a safety net (By turning uphill), they can bail out of the calamity. Do repeat the J-turn drill several more times to help concur the fears. Another exercise that you can do is do it on a less-steep terrain. Be sure to check their *turn shapes* and their balance on the skis to determine why the child is picking up so much speed (See figure 6).[5, 16] Do you know how the different-shaped turns affect speed? How does S-shaped curve, a C-shaped, or J-shaped curve, affect speed? What about different size pizzas (See figure 7)? What about pizzas versus parallel platform (See figure 10)? Some of the other fears besides speed, are heights and jumps. One of the things that I tell my students is, *"Speed causes injuries. That is why they have safe speed limits in the city and on the highways. When your parents exceed the speed limits, they can get a speeding ticket and you can get one too from the snow patrol. So, always ski safely by going slow."* There are several ways of implementing **speed control:**

The student should only use terrain steepness that matches his/her skill level.

Apply the J-turns to go the slowest and come to a stop after the turn.

Apply the C-turns to go at moderate speeds.

Apply the S-turns to go at faster speeds.

The student must finish the turns for the different shaped turns to work.

Use the wedge turns rather than the parallel platform to go slower. Use the entire hill by traversing the entire hill and adjusting the speed by going uphill or going downhill. Doing Garlands across the hill is a great way to practice the three skills: edging-, pressure-, and rotary-control to help control speed.

Do spend the time to inform the adaptive children to not bomb the hill at Mache 2 speeds because of dire consequences.

Fear of speed is one of the major reasons the adaptive child loses speed control because instinct causes them to lean back, thinking that that will slow them down—wrong!

Chapter 10
Developing Good Sportsmanship

No skiing manual teaches the fundamentals of good sportsmanship, the focus is only on the mechanics and techniques of the sport. In all sports, including skiing, it is a lost art and seems to be getting worse as time goes by. It is time that we add this to our teaching schedule for the special needs students. What is the definition of good sportsmanship? There are many definitions, but it revolves around some basic principles listed below:

Treat everyone with respect; no teasing or making fun of a classmate or opponent.

Be always supportive to everyone; always provide positive comments of encouragements.

Always be fair and ethical to everyone.

Be polite, gracious, and caring to others.

Be courteous and helpful to everyone around you.

Always have a positive attitude no matter what the circumstances are; no one wants to be around individuals who complain continuously.

Practice self-control always, despite failures; no temper tantrums. When a fellow ski student fails, encourage him/her with helpful and caring comments of inspiration so they can become better skiers. Always show humility when you excel at a new technique; be humble always.

Don't be a poor sport and give up the drill or exercise when it doesn't go correctly; don't give up, persevere.

Win with dignity. Follow the rules of the game without exception.

Lose with grace; do not make an ugly scene after the game in public. As their ski coach, fill the children with disabilities, with heartful goodwill so they can share it with their friends on and off the ski slopes. There are so many issues that deter us from getting the kids to become better sportsmen/sportswomen. We all need to be more diligent and not sit on the sideline to achieve this goal of teaching children to change their attitudes and coach them the many ways to become better sportsmen/sportswomen.

Emphasize to the kids we should continuously point the moral and ethical compass to True North. As ski coaches we are obligated to teach these special needs children the fundamentals of good conduct, so they can mature in adults that are, honest, transparent, kind, respectful and helpful. We should not be myopic and focus only on the mechanics and techniques of adaptive skiing; we should actively teach the fundamentals of good sportsmanship.

For example, an advanced -level performance adaptive skier is having difficulties with making smooth turns. His friend said to him you look like Rob the robot! The adaptive coach, went over to Rob the robot, and corrected him by saying, *"Now was that very nice what you said to your best friend; how would you feel if he said that to you?"* I said, *"Don't be a poor sportsman; instead treat him like a real friend should be treated by being kind, supportive, and helpful."* I said, *"I'll help both of you; and you help one another!"*

Chapter 11

Where to get Specialized Adaptive Assistance

There are many places when you can get assistance for your special needs child. The Park City Ability Center in Park City, Utah and Snowmass Ski Resort in Vail, Colorado are great adaptive resource centers. A brief listing of places where you can get help:

Breckenridge Outdoor Education Center: Adaptive Ski and Ride School; Breckenridge, Colorado. They have the latest equipment.

National Sports Center for the Disabled; Winter Park, Colorado.

Steamboat Adaptive Recreational Sports; Steamboat Springs, Colorado.

Oregon Adaptive Sports; Bend, Oregon.

Jackson Hole Adaptive Mountain Sports School; Jackson Hole, Wyoming.

New England Disabled Sports; Lincoln, New Hampshire.

Achieve Tahoe, Tahoe, California.

Maine Adaptive Sports and Recreation; Newey, Maine

Adaptive Sports Program in New Mexico; Santa Fe, New Mexico.

Three Trackers at Boston Mills Ski Resort, Peninsula, Ohio.

Adaptive Sports at Sun Peak; Sun Peaks; Vancouver, British Columbia.

Mountain Access; Hamilton, Ontario.

Snowmass Ski Resorts; Vail, Colorado.

All of these adaptive skiing resorts have these-specialized equipment and PSIA certified adaptive instructors. Call ahead and find out the amenities that they provide for special needs individuals.

Chapter 12
Summary

Special needs children are very special people, and they deserve the very best treatment, care, and skiing instructions. It starts with building trust and bonding with them. Be mindful that safety is your highest priority when teaching these special kids. Keep them safe by teaching the ABCs of safety, which is only the beginning. Check to see if your students understand what and how to implement the safety code. Know each type of disorder in depth and apply the information into your lesson plans. Apply the Ski Concept Model[25] and Five Fundamentals of Skiing Model[25] into your skiing instructions. Know the different types of ski tools and equipment and use them to your advantage.

Children are made for fun. Use the many games and tools to create fun and lasting memories. Be a resource for the parents when it comes to recommending centers of excellence for these adaptive children. Be able to teach all performance levels (Beginner, Intermediate, Advance) with a passion. Take these special needs children on a journey that they will never forget.

Photo 84. An exuberant little boy with a rare-childhood neurological disorder called childhood-Parkinson Disease. Despite his handicap, he made it to the top of the mountain through sheer determination, which made him feel on top of the world.

Welcome to the Exciting world of adaptive skiing!

References

Adaptive Alpine Technical Manual; PSIA Education Foundation, Lakewood, Colorado, 2017; 230 pages.

Adaptive Instruction Supplement: Diagnosis and Medication Classifications; PSIA Education Foundation, Lakewood, Colorado, 2019; 80 pages.

Adaptive Snowsports Instruction; PSIA Education Foundation, Lakewood, Colorado, 2003; 108 pages.

Adult Alpine Teaching Handbook; PSIA; Vail and Beaver Creek Ski &Snowboard Schools; Beaver Creek, Colorado, 2011; 318 pages. Alpine Handbook; PSIA Educational Foundation; Lakewood, Colorado,1996; 77 pages.

Alpine & Snowboard Teaching Handbook; Vail Resorts Management Co.; Vail, Colorado, 2004; 200 pages.

Alpine Technical Manual; PSIA; PSIA/AASI American Snowsports Education Foundation, Inc.; Lakewood, Colorado, 2014; 150 pages.

Brocksmith, Blake, Dorfman, Gary, and Lichterman, Douglas; How to Play Harmonica: A Complete Guide for Beginners; Adams Media; New York, New York, 2018; 175 pages.

Children's Alpine Teaching Handbook; PSIA/AASI Intermountain (Northwest); American Snowsports Education Association; Lakewood, Colorado, 2010; 314 pages.

Children's Instruction Manual; PSIA Education Foundation; 1997; 151 pages.

Children's Instruction Manual, 2nd Ed.; PSIA Education Foundation; Lakewood, Colorado, 2008; 128 pages.

Core Concepts for Snowsports Instructors: Teaching; PSIA/AASI Education Foundation; Lakewood, Colorado, 2008; 90 pages.

Cues to Ineffective and Effective Teaching; American Snowsports Education Foundation; PSIA, Educational Foundation, Lakewood, Colorado, 2008; 12 pages.

Herrin, Nicholas; "PSIA-AASI's Commitment to Snowsports Education: Is outlined in Best Practices for Teaching During COVIID-19"; 32 Degrees; American Snowsports Education Foundation; Lakewood, Colorado, Fall 2020; pages 45-47.

Jay, Joshua; "Magic: The Complete Course; Workman Publishing Company; New York, New York, 2008; 288. Pages.

Kazanjian, Kirk; Exceeding Customer Expectation; Random House Publishing; New York, New York, 2007; 256 pages.

Maslow, A.; "A Theory of Human Motivation; Psychological Review; 50:370-396 (1943).

New Snowsports Instructor Guide; PSIA/AASI Intermountain (West); PSIA Education Foundation; Lakewood, Colorado, Colorado, 2018; 27 pages.

Park and Pipe Instructor's Guide: Freestyle; PSIA/AASI American Snowsports Education Foundation, 2005; 156 pages.

Pogue, David; "Magic for Dummies"; IDG Books Worldwide, Inc; New York, New York, 1998; 369 pages.

Snowboard Teaching Handbook; Product number 121PSIA Education Foundation; Lakewood, Colorado, 2015; 358 pages.

Stadelman, Paul and Fife, Bruce; "Ventriloquism Made Easy"; Piccadilly Books, Ltd.; Colorado Springs, Colorado, 2003; 108 pages.

Stanbury, John B., Wyngaarden, James B., Fredrickson, Donald S., Goldstein, Joseph, L., and Brown, Michael S., The Metabolic Basis of Inherited Disease; McGraw-Hill 1983 (5th edition); New York, New York.

Trueman, Bob; Ski in Control—How to Ski Any Piste Anywhere in Full Control: Man, Woman, Young or Old; Trueman Publishing Company, Roland Heights, California, 2017; 142 pages.

Teaching Snowsports Manual; American Snowsports Education Association, Inc. Lakewood, Colorado, 1918; 262 pages.

Vail and Beaver Creek Children's Alpine Teaching Handbook; Vail Resorts Management Co.; Vail Colorado, 2004; 200 pages.

Wahlba, A., and Bridgewell, L. "Maslow Reconsidered: A Review of Research on the Need of Hierarchy Theory; Organizational Research and Human Performance; 15: 212-240 (1976).

2020 Ski Instructor Guide; Deer Valley Ski Resort; Deer Valley, Utah, 2019; 206 pages.

2020 ADA Standards of Medical Care in Diabetes; American Medical Association, Muncie, Indiana, 2019; 206 pages.

Notes

[←1]

https://disabledATSdisabledsportseasternsierra.org

Alpine Skiing/Snowboarding Model

[←2]

Ski Resorts Adjust, Hope Season Gets a Longer Run, "in USA Today, November 19, 2020, page 4D."

[←3]

THE US Review of Books

5.0 ★★★★★★

How to Create Fun for Children with Disabilities on the Ski Slopes

by Dr. Herbert K. Naito

book review by Toby Berry

"Every person is special."

In this book, readers discover how to make a physically rigorous sport like skiing fun for children with disabilities. They gain insights into how the American education system approaches the education of disabled children. Readers who will be teaching and coaching disabled children are encouraged to use the CAP (cognitive, affective, physical) model, which revolves around a child's developmental stages. The book looks at various age groups and provides ideas and approaches for working with each one. Colorful graphics also accompany the well-detailed narratives, which blend personal and professional reflections. The book also discusses the importance of incorporating arts like coloring into one's ski lesson plans. Additionally, the text provides a careful overview of how to work with a range of disabilities, including autism spectrum disorder and cognitive impairment disorders.

Naito's book is effective because of its accessibility. Readers who are either inexperienced or experienced in this particular area of coaching will appreciate the information this book provides. What also makes the work special is that the lessons and ide as it provides are useful not only in the realm of skiing but also in the educational classroom. Most of all, the ideas provided in this book will help coaches encourage their students to go beyond simply becoming good athletes. It helps them encourage their students to develop into thoughtful individuals who possess self-awareness and consideration for others. An emphasis on safety also centers the book. Moreover, it emphasizes the necessity for patience when working with children of any ability. Most importantly, Naito's book encourages readers to embrace a particularly special calling in the skiing world.